SPECTOR BOOKS

Joseph Grigely
Christina Irrgang
Daniela Stöppel

on Fari Shams'

EUROPEAN CIVILIZATION, PETER THE GREAT, AND THE ORDER OF THINGS

ABC: generated with reference to the alphabetical order of image titles

DD: generated with reference to Diderot's Map of the System of Human Knowledge

MA: generated with reference to the system of Michel Adanson for the classification of plants in Senegal

TABLE OF CONTENTS

Morad Montazami
Preface 6

A lecture by John Merriman on Peter the Great and the Territorial Expansion of Russia followed by an alphabetical list of chosen keywords 9

Index of images 20

Alphabetic list of image titles 31

Plates [MA] 33

Joseph Grigely
Reading Rectangles 37

Plates [MA] 45

Exhibition views 49

Christina Irrgang
Visueller Totalität Begegnen 53

Plates [DD / MA] 61

Daniela Stöppel
Peter der Große und die Ordnung seiner Welt 69

Michel Adanson's system of classification of plants in Senegal described by Michel Foucault 74

Diderot Map of the System of Human Knowledge 75

Plates [ABC / DD / MA] 77

English Translations
Christina Irrgang: Encountering Visual Totality 86
Daniela Stöppel: Peter the Great and the order of his world 93

Contributors 98

Imprint 100

Morad Montazami

PREFACE

Fari Shams' *European Civilization Peter the Great and the Order of Things* project or apparatus presents itself in various ways: as an art installation (as such, no aesthetic or poetic claim should be denied to it), as an interactive processor for historical and contemporary systems of knowledge, and, finally, as a post-Internet speculative data calculator. It is not the role of the artist to impose one function upon our experience as a reader or spectator, but she may certainly entertain a certain level of complexity in order to decipher these different functions. In a way, this gives to the viewer the responsibility to define their own relation to spectatorship.

The term "spectator" now has an obsolete connotation: it is out of touch with the contemporary burning questions about the democratisation of "public collections", the access to sources, and the constitution of immaterial heritage. We have lost count of the various devices utilised by the museum to "include the visitor in a unique experience", possibly invite them to "share a moment of conviviality" or "political and citizen awareness", and moreover "to welcome all subjectivities" that refound the museum on its intrinsic use value and its ability to submit to all criticism. Just as the museum is today subject to the immaterial value of artistic innovations and the hybridisation of knowledge systems and networks through artistic practices, the images appearing in Fari Shams' apparatus oscillate between archival data, plain pictures and dialectical documents.

The wisest museums wishing to cross the threshold of presentism and the overabundance of crisis factors must expose and publicise the anchoring of their collections in an imperialist history that served a meaning of "culture" — as well as an education of the eye — defined by the valorisation of objects captured, deterritorialised and robbed from colonised or enemy territories. These "other" objects, often magnified by a sophisticated museum mise-en-scène which Fari Shams' apparatus debunks completely, ultimately embodied the dismantling logic upon which the museum was based in colonial times — a logic in which the museum itself becomes the object in our post-critical era (an era made of dominant self-critical discourses and strategies of inculpability). The signs of such a process are emerging in our time: as we discuss not just the museum's duty to return certain objects from the African continent, but also the museum as a hub, "social network", or "soft power" — terms that denote the museum's insistence on coming out of self-defined limits and, like the internet, connecting everywhere and to everyone.

By submitting to the double criticism of the postcolonial paradigm and the "usage" or the digital revolution, the museum, in a way, adapts itself to an ever more delocalised and globalised cultural industry, one that is both intangible and accumulative. A dematerialised cultural industry in which the value of the work of art progressively tends to be indexed not only through its high-resolution data, but also the global circulation of digital image banks or documents that related originally to collections that were first and foremost based on nationalist borders and political systems. There remains hardly anyone who might themselves be astonished at the ecological, patrimonial, migratory, or even democratic crises that today make up the daily bread of many museums and biennials of contemporary art. The abundance of these diffuse crises have magnified the concept of the mirror-museum: one which reflects every jolt of society through the most varied or the most standardised artistic tendencies. As in a cabinet of curiosities, everything must enter the museum, but we do not know on what grounds the museum can stabilise itself. We could even add: everything is in the museum, but the museum is in nothing. As such, it becomes a platform of communication and archival devices rather than an institution in the classic sense of the word. On the one hand, the stories told by museums are increasingly more inclusive and less elitist; on the other hand, we find museums rooted not as much in history (or even multiple micro-histories) as they are in iconographic ecosystems and in geocultural algorithms. Nothing, however, prevents the museum from being both the site of a major epistemological dismantling, aided especially by the postcolonial turn and the digital age, and the dematerialised receptacle of a spectacle that, however captivating, is disturbing; at the museum, the myths of high resolution or connectivity and that of interchangeable or hybrid identities prevail in the most indecipherable duality.

In such a complex chaotic horizon of local micro-politics and global data struggles, Fari Shams' art of the post-Internet apparatus shows us that randomness is not always entropic and that neither transmission nor becoming an actor-editor is always consensual.

John Merriman

EUROPEAN CIVILIZATION 1648-1945[1]

Lecture 4 - Peter the Great

Territorial

empire

empires

empires

empire

empire.

Empire

empire

empire

empires

empire

territorial

Mongols

Istanbul

Black Sea

Georgia

territorial

Georgians

Black Sea

Black Sea

River

port

Black Sea

empire

empire

empire

empire

empire

Russo-

Japanese War

tortured

science

astrolabes sailing

port sailing sailing

observatories hospitals botanical gardens gardens

botanical gardens

Church Church

geography maps map making

trade

military power military power

European culture

traditional

westernizers

westernizers

west-

ernizers

Peasant

roasts fancy
parties

generosity

tortured
tortured
torture

empire

peasant

dressing up
dressing fancy clothes worn
boots

hat

ordinary
people
carriages carriage
carriage
eating
walking
Russian,
wooden peasant house

peasants

port

fancy lodgings

Louvre palace museum

ships
eating
peasant cabbage soup porridge meat pickled cucumbers ham and cheese

wine wine

wine
eating eating
ordinary people
wine

ordinary people peasant
dress sailor
fake names

portraits

books

eating drinking

dressing up

fancy dances fancy people

fire-fighting

fireworks explosives cannon fire reli-
gious singing chess
billiards mathematical instruments
telescopes
globes
mapped

Tradition

private library

books fortifications hydraulics artillery navigation shipbuilding

books

tradition

scientific revolution Enlightenment

Royal Society

scientific revolution

sciences Sciences

tradition law school medical school

books

church

empire

port

navy

navy port port

navy navy rivers

carpentry Medical School
dissected bodies Thames
port shipbuilding
ships rationality
scientific revolution
scientific revolution

navy river

navy

traditional
empire

empire

empire

traditional
churches Church
urban planning

churches state structures
Madrid Berlin Versailles

Haussmann
imperialism large boulevards armies
reviewing stands

dress western Euro-
pean women beards
shave beards

church

western style wigs
Versailles high heels
high heels European style dresses

traditional

peasant

tortured
torture torture

books
church
scientific revolution

marble work metal
work copper work shipbuilding

scientific cul-
ture rationality Enlightenment
church

science

ships ships

museum naviga-

tion books pamphlets prints

maps

tradition traditional

westernizers

Enlightenment

1 – Open Yale Courses. *HIST202:EUROPEAN CIVILIZATION, 1648-1945, Lecture4, Peter the Great.* Online Lecture. https://oyc.yale.edu/history/hist-202/lecture-4, accessed 29/09/2013.

Only the keywords chosen from the lecture for the purposes of this project are shown here since the permission to publish the full transcript of it was denied by the copyright holder.

ALPHABETICAL LIST OF CHOSEN KEYWORDS FROM LECTURE

Armies
Artillery
Astrolabes
Battered hat
Beards
Berlin
Billiards
Black sea
Books
Botanical gardens
Cabbage soup
Cannon fire
Carpentry
Carriages
Chess
Churches
Cobblestones and high heels
Copper work
Dancing
Dissecting bodies
Drinking
Drums
Eating
Empire
Enlightenment
European culture
Explosives
Fake names
Fancy clothes
Fancy dances
Fancy lodgings
Fancy people
Fire fighting
Fireworks
Fortifications
Gardens
Generosity
Geography
Globes
Georgia
Ham and cheese
High heels
Hospitals
Hydraulics
Imperialism
Istanbul
Lakes
Large boulevards
Law school
London Thames
Louvre palace
Madrid
Map making
Maps
Marble work
Mathematical instruments
Maths
Medical school
Metal work
Military bases
Military power
Mongols
Museum
Navigation
Navy
Observatories
Ordinary people
Pamphlets
Parties
Peasants
Peasant lodgings
Pickled cucumbers
Ponds
Porridge
Port
Portraits
Post Haussmann
Paris
Prints
Private library
Rationality
Religious singing
Reviewing stands
Rise and fall of empires
Rivers
Roasts
Royal society
Russian peasant house
Russo Japanese war 1904-05
Sailing
Sailor
Science
Scientific culture
Scientific revolution
Shaving
Shipbuilding
Ships
State structures
Telescopes
Tension with Westernizers
Territorial size
Torture
Trade
Tradition
Urban planning
Versailles
Walking
Wealth
Western European dress
Western style wigs
Wine
Worn boots

INDEX

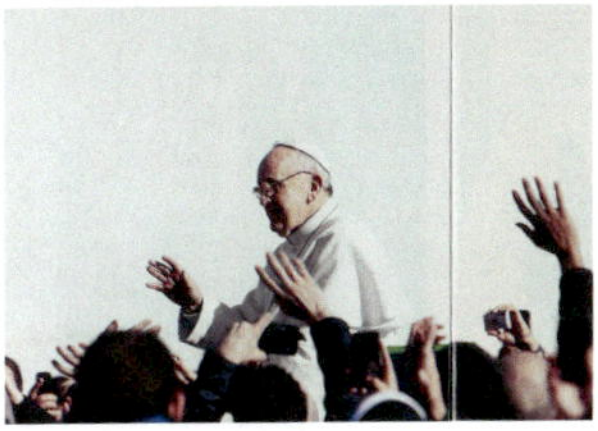
001

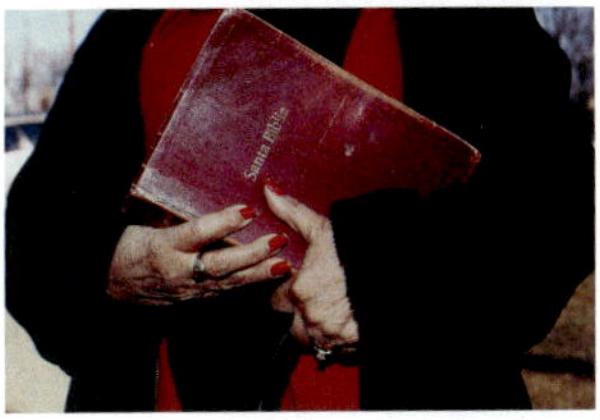
002

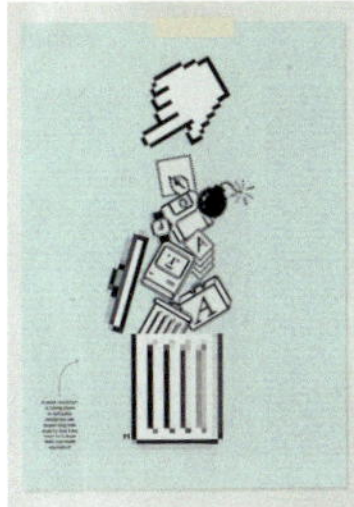
003

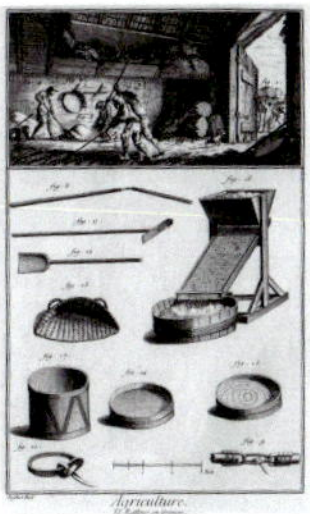

004

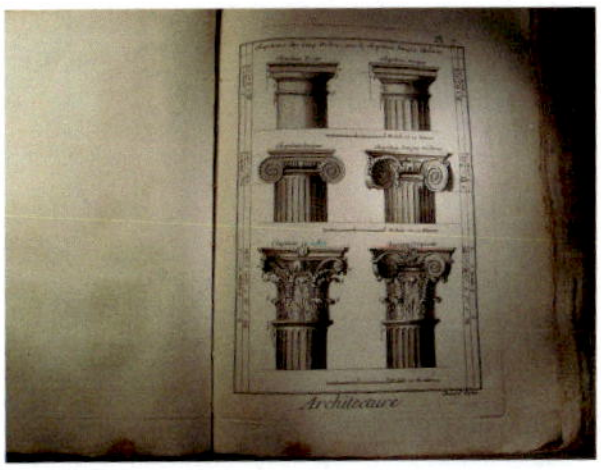

005

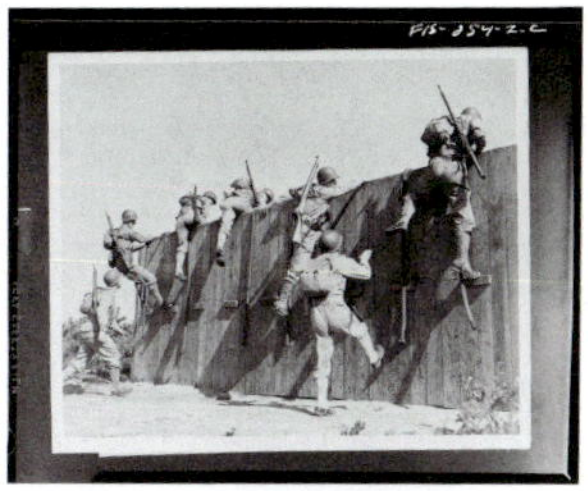
006

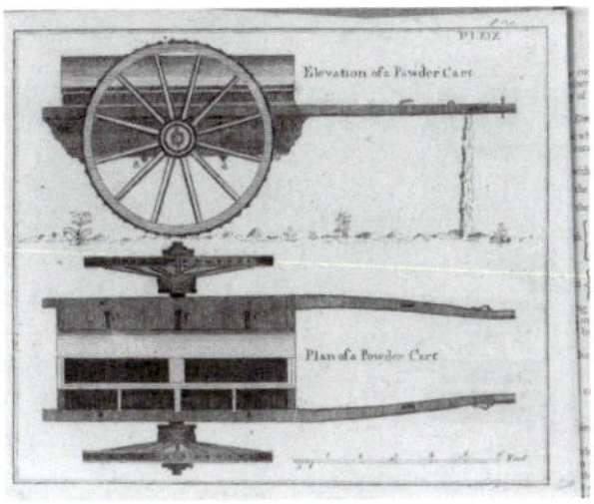

007

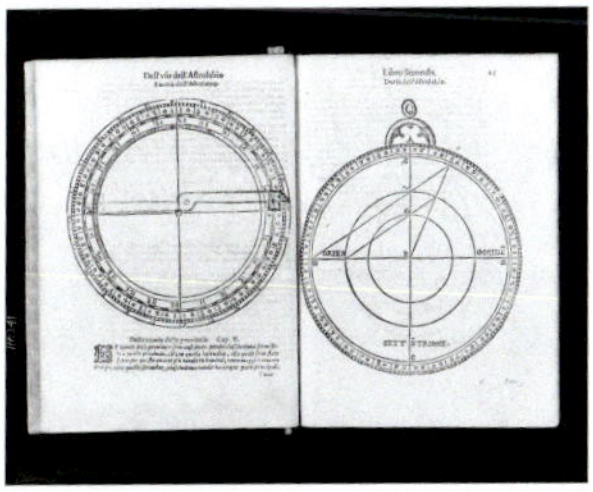
008

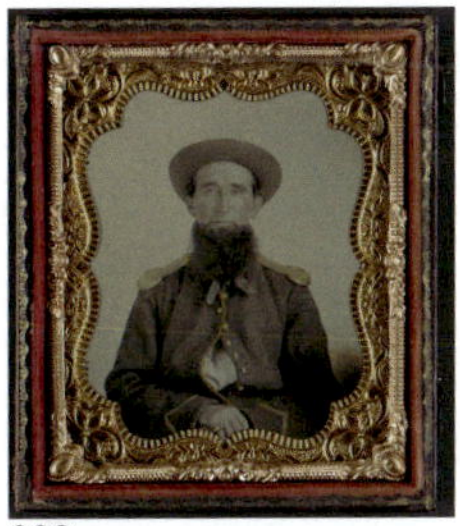
009

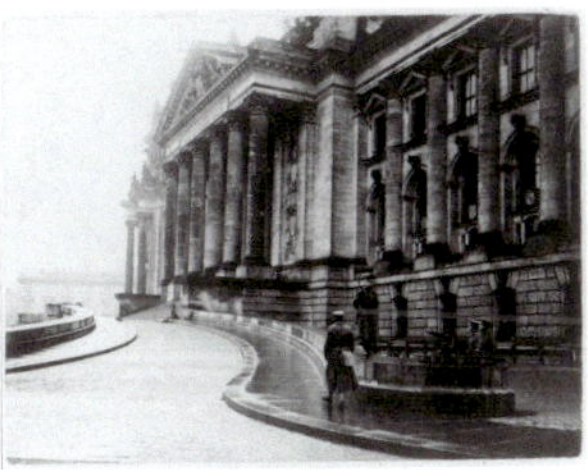
010

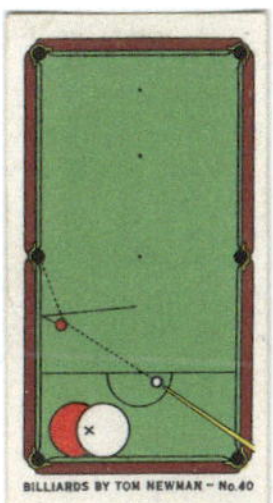

011

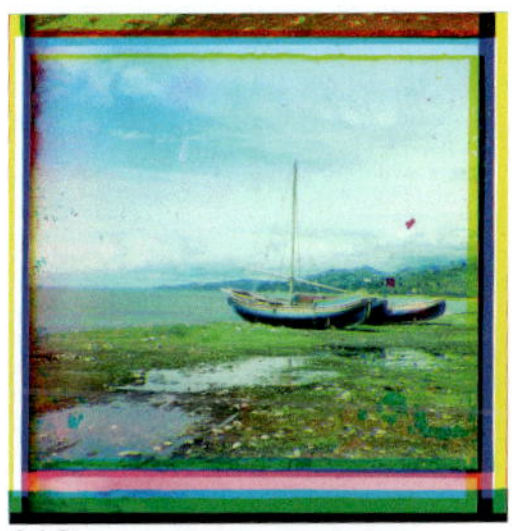
012

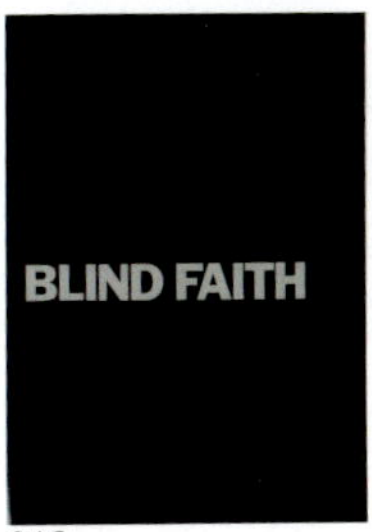

013

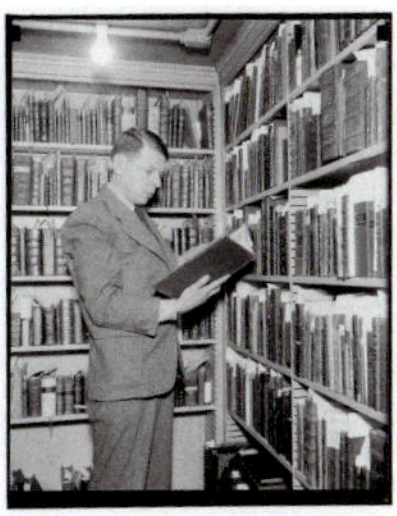
014

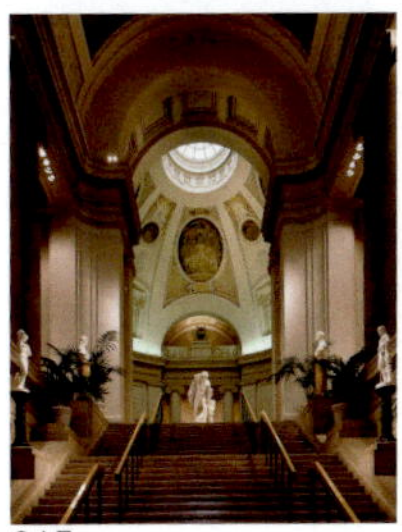
015

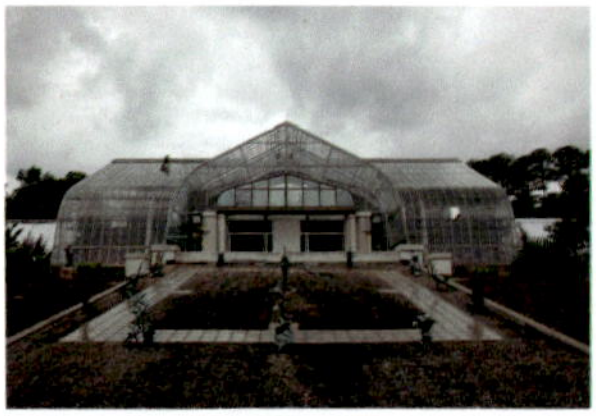

016

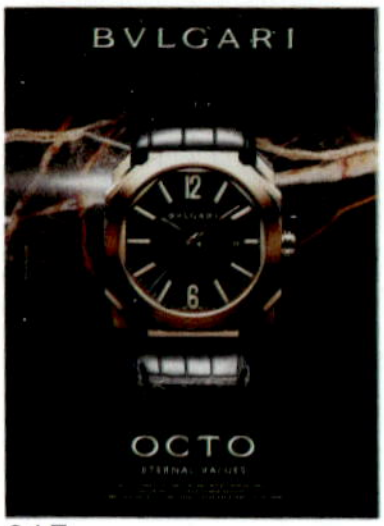

017

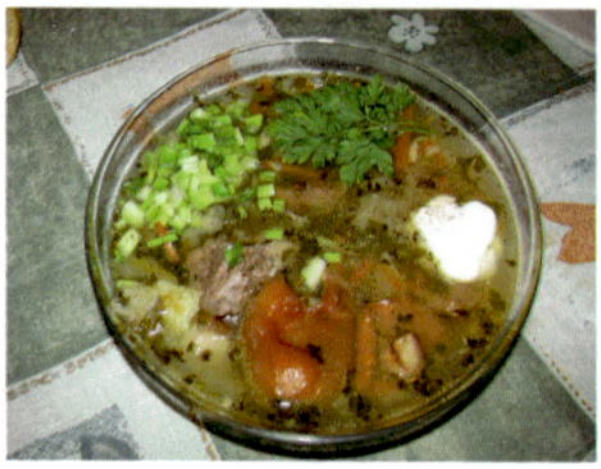

018

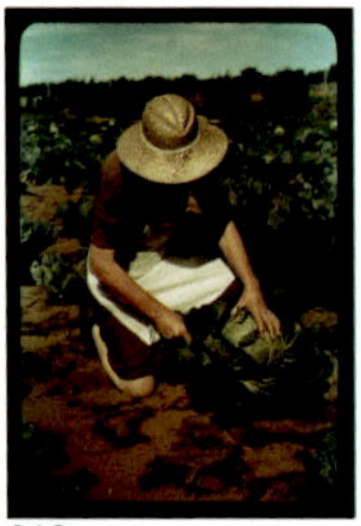

019

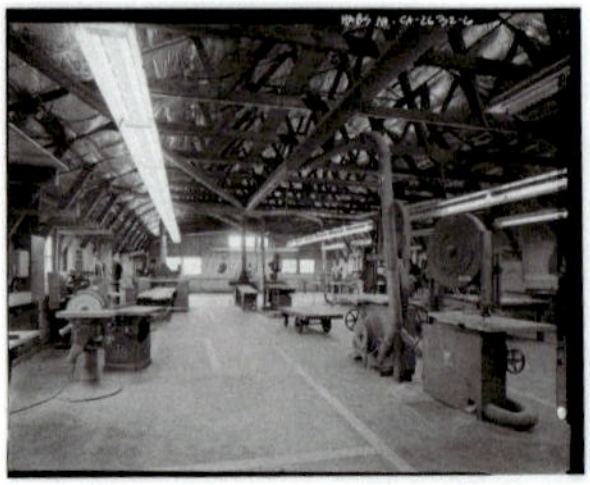

020

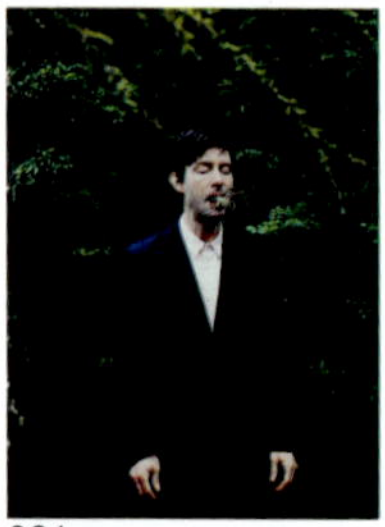

021

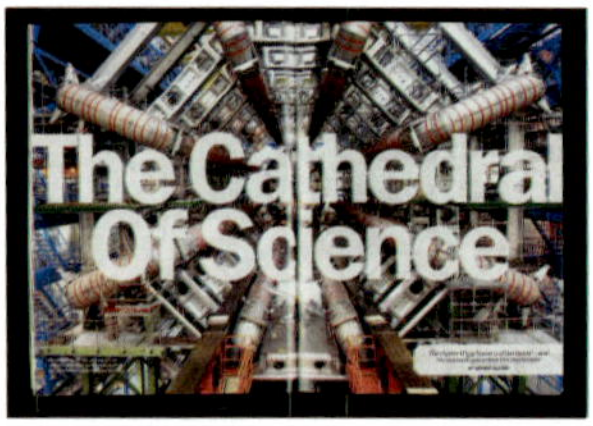

022

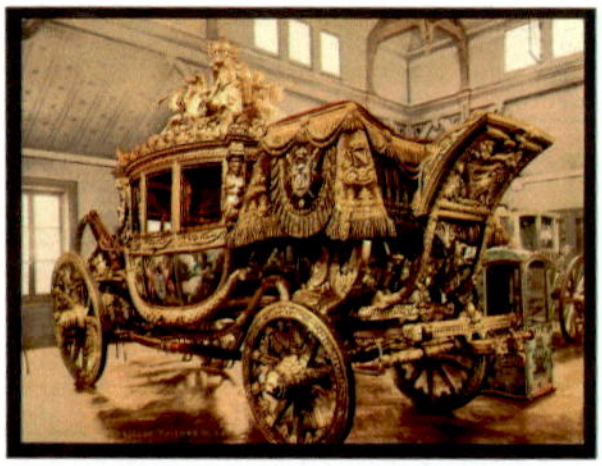

023

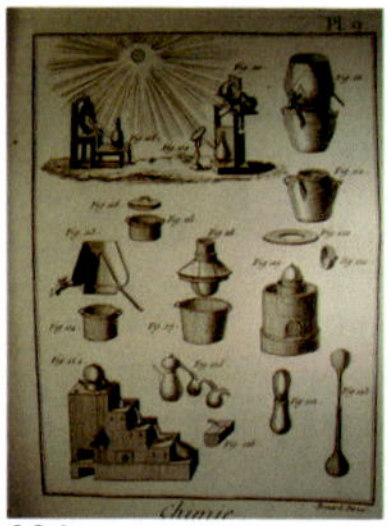

024

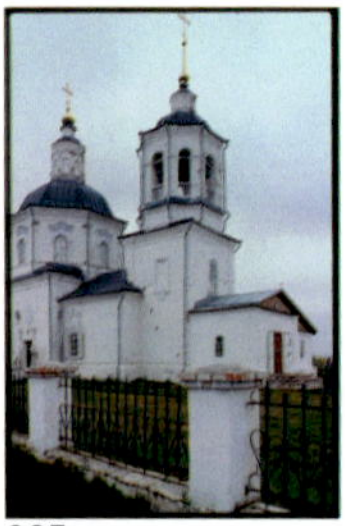

025

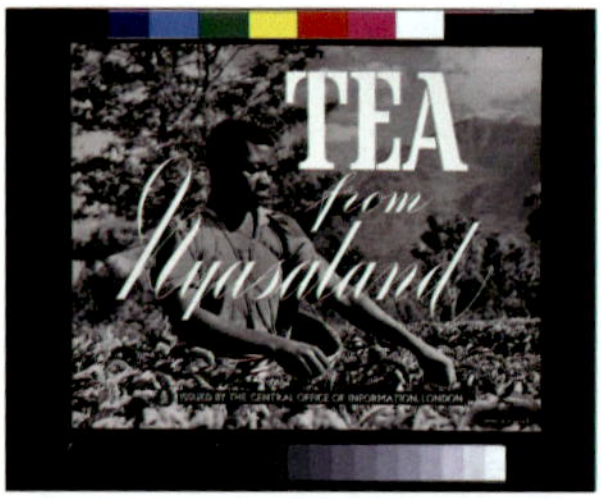

026

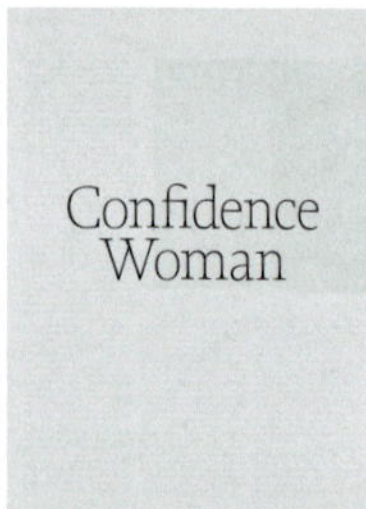

027

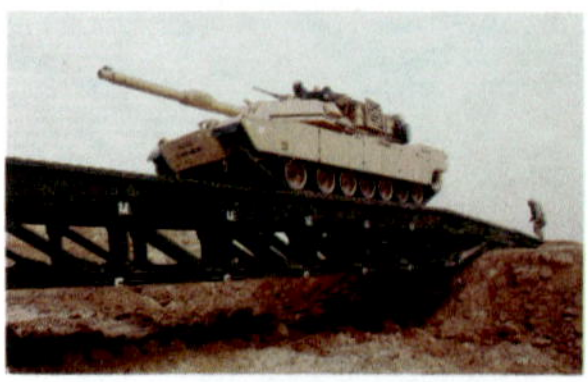

028

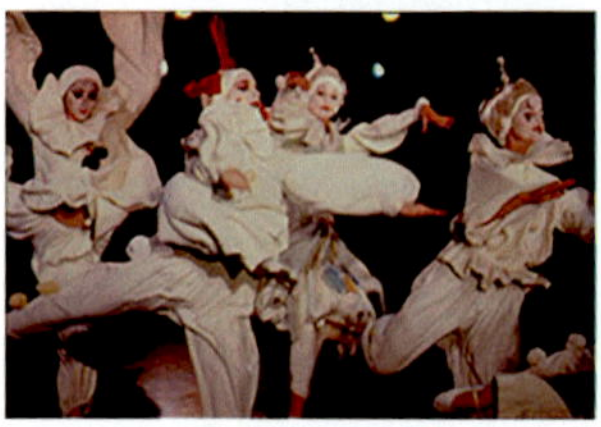

029

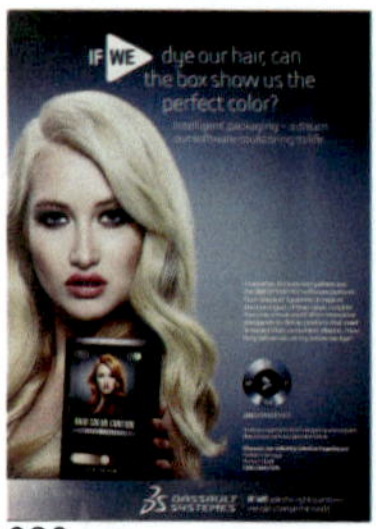

030

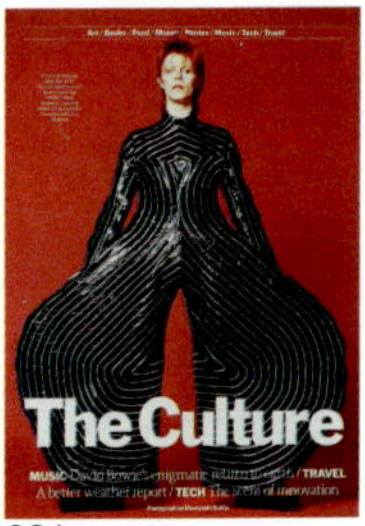

031

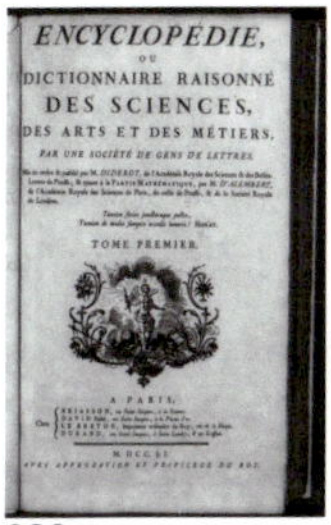

032

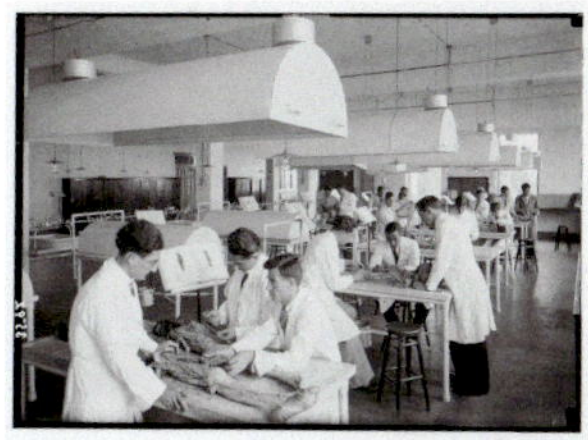
033

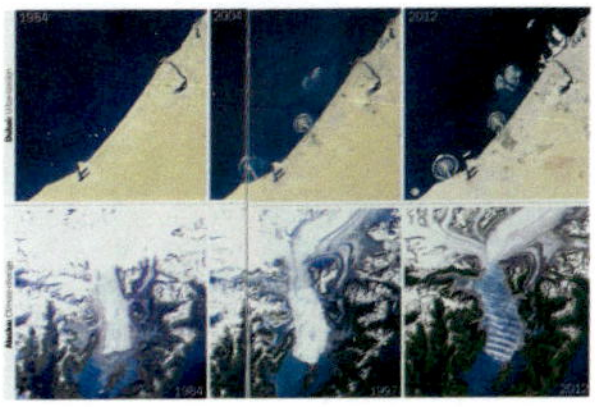
034

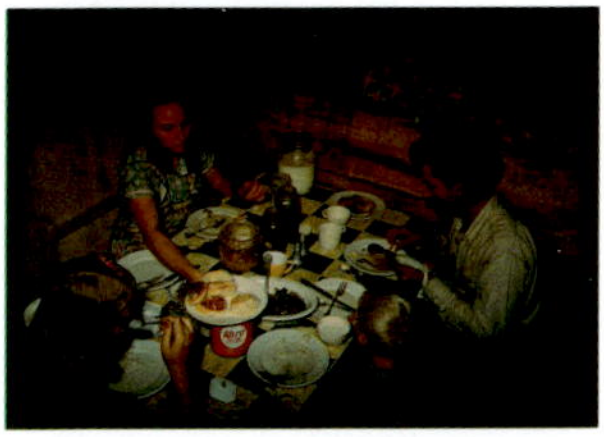
035

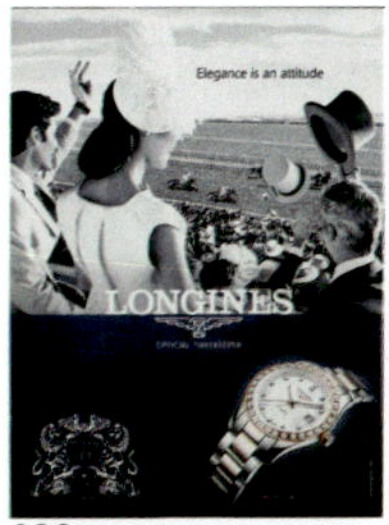

036

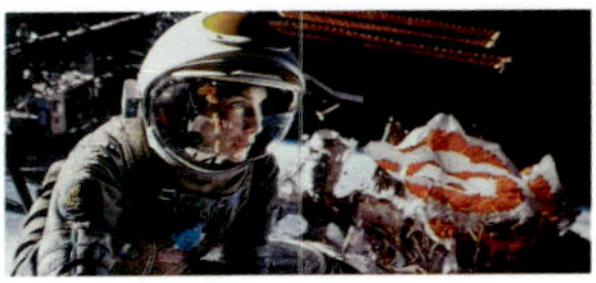
037

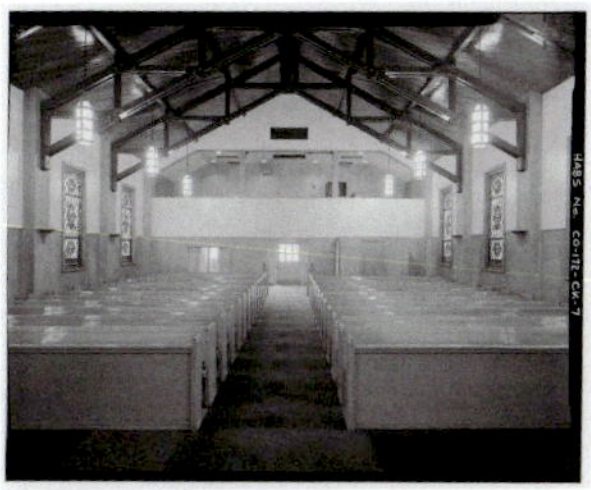
038

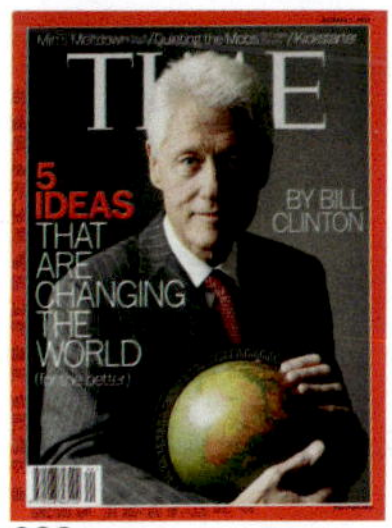

039

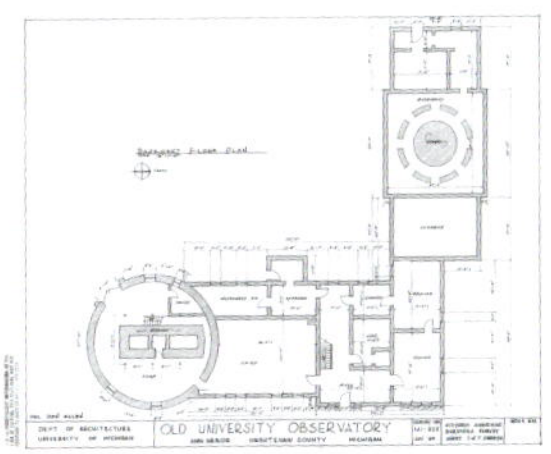

040

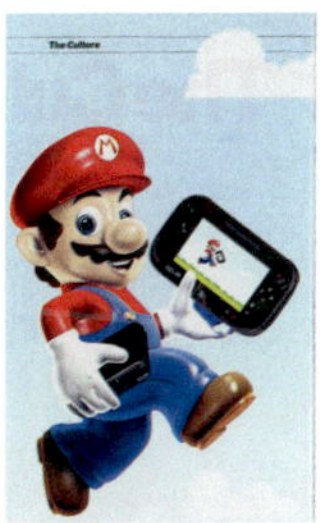

041

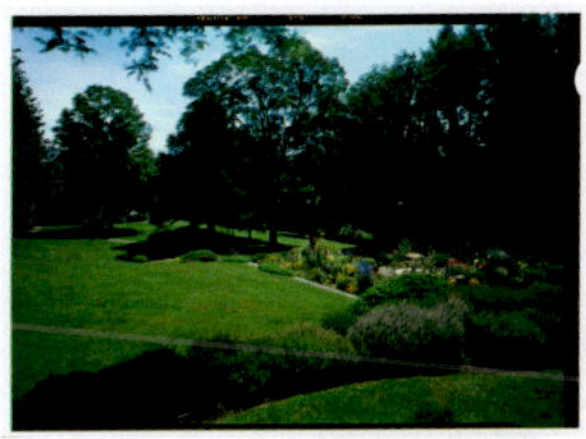
042

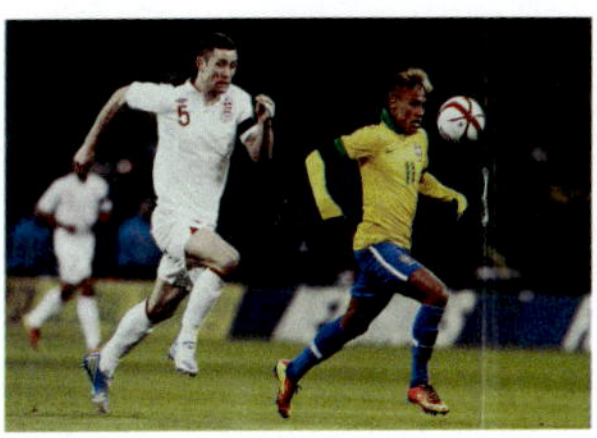
043

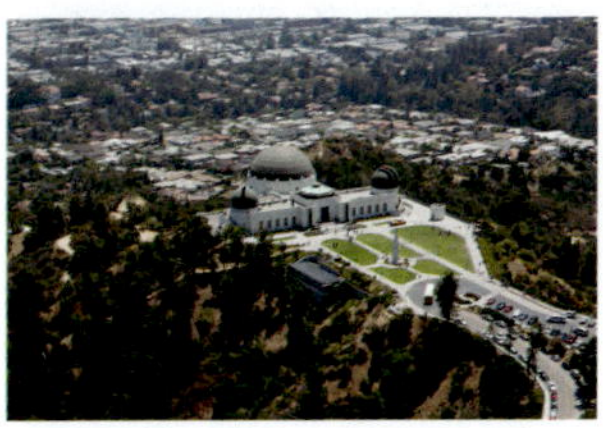
044

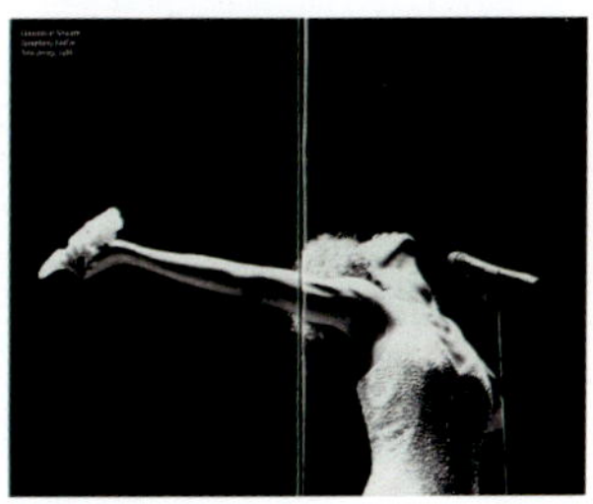
045

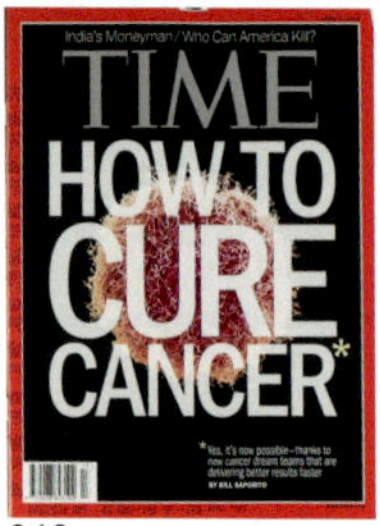

046

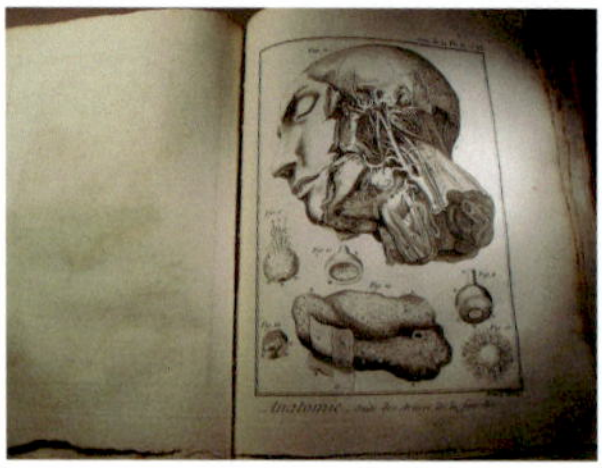
047

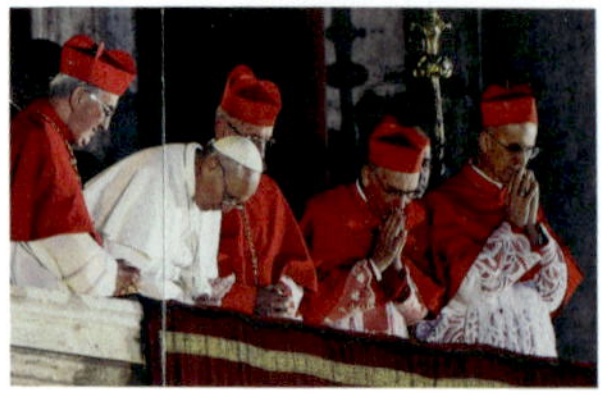
048

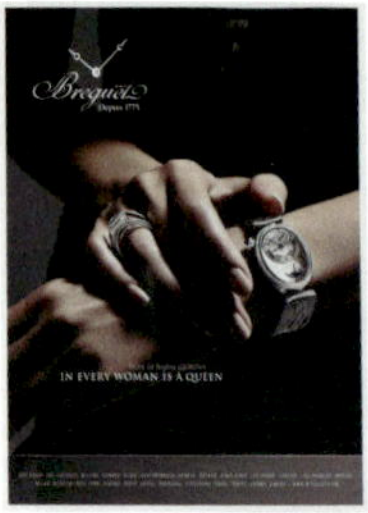

049

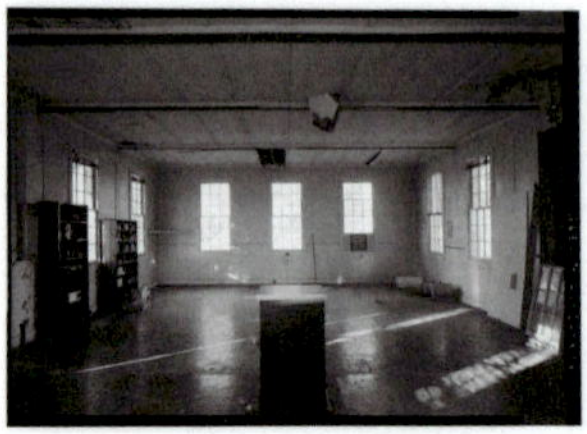
050

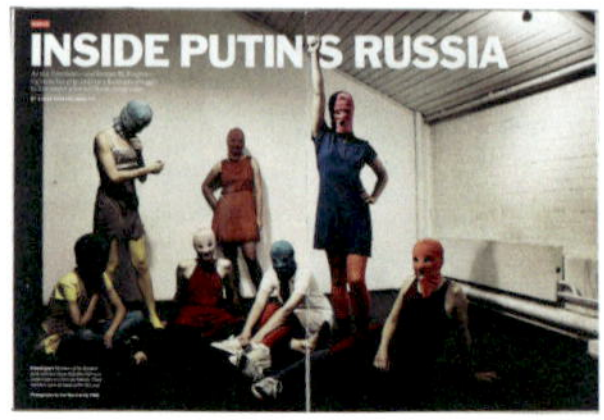

051

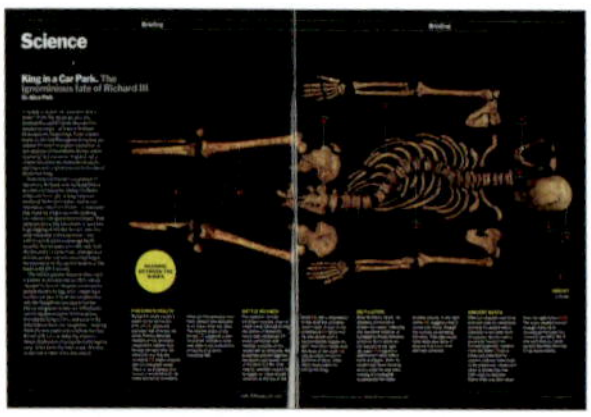

052

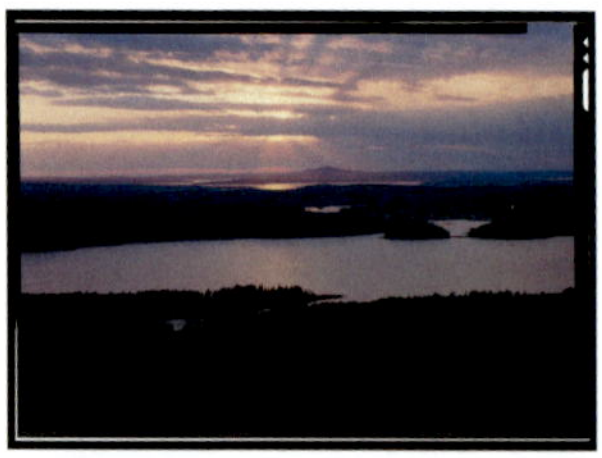
053

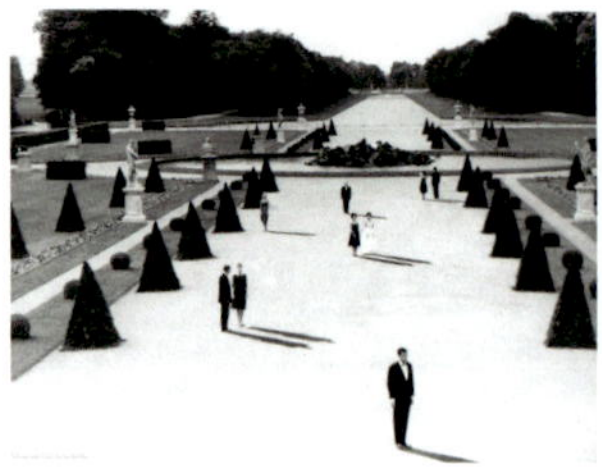
054

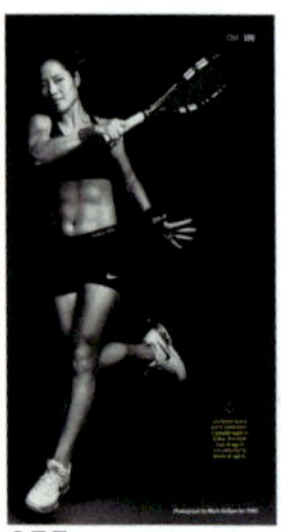
055

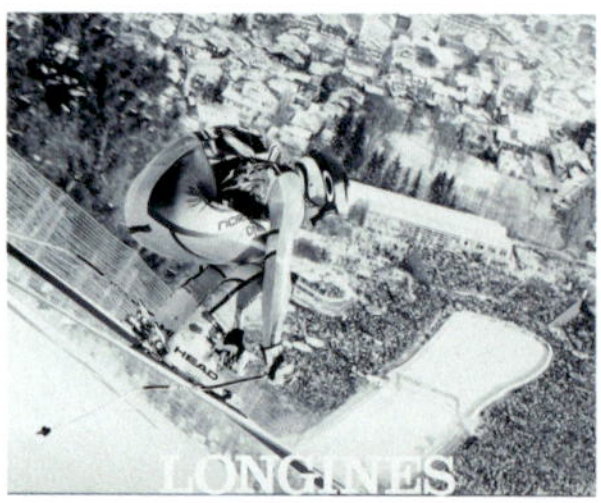

056

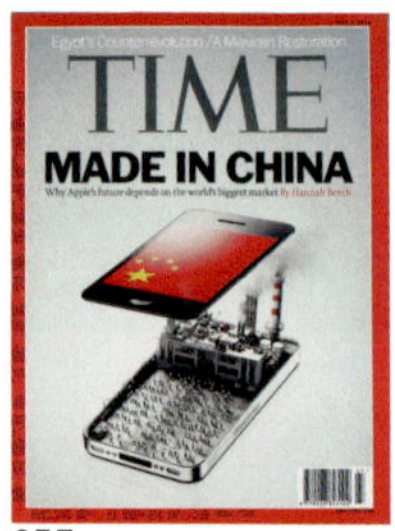

057

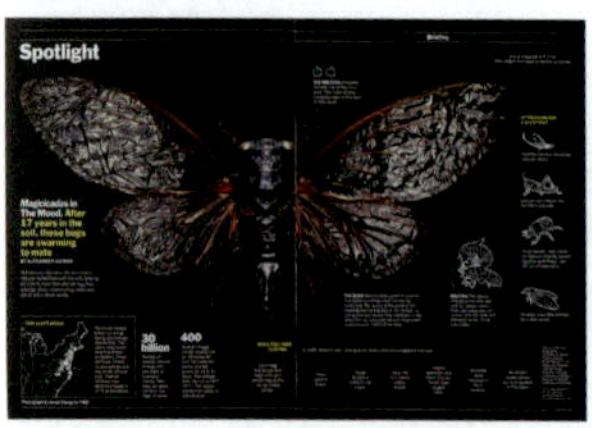

058

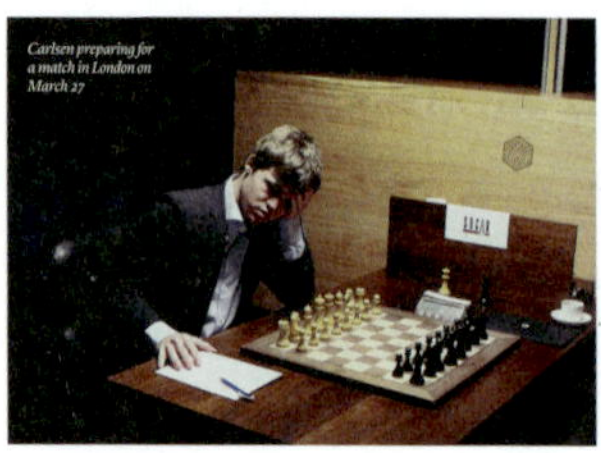

059

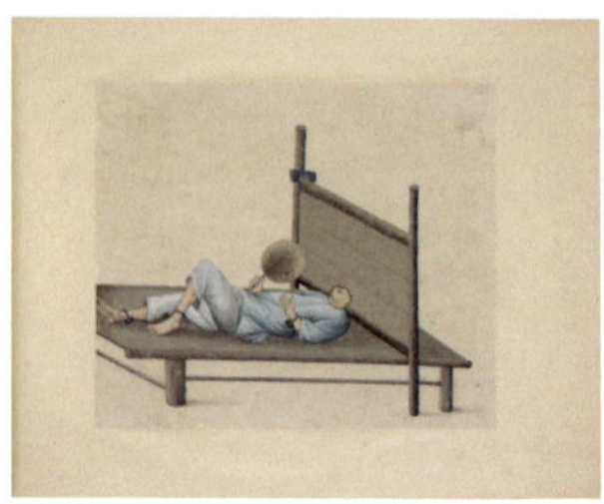
060

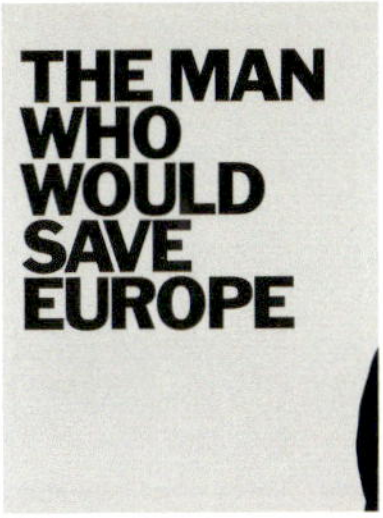

061

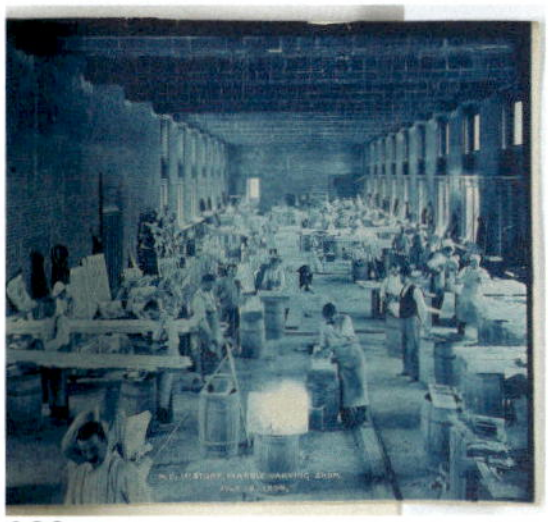

062

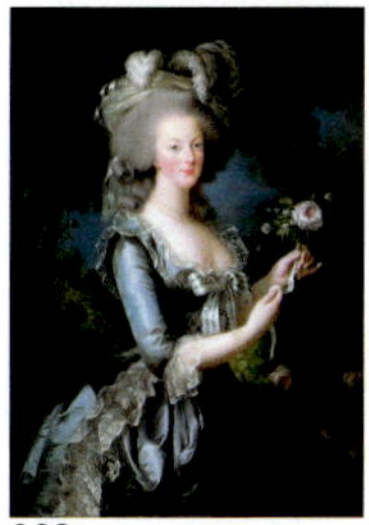

063

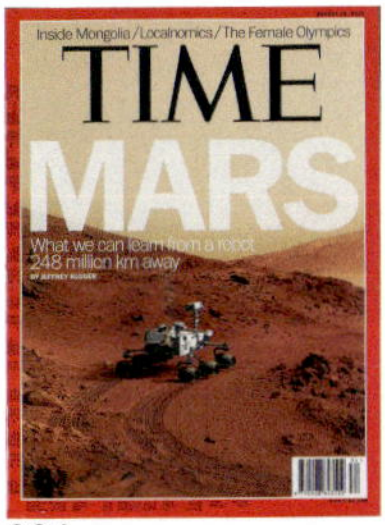

064

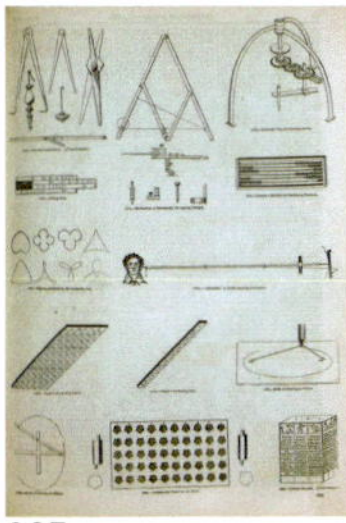

065

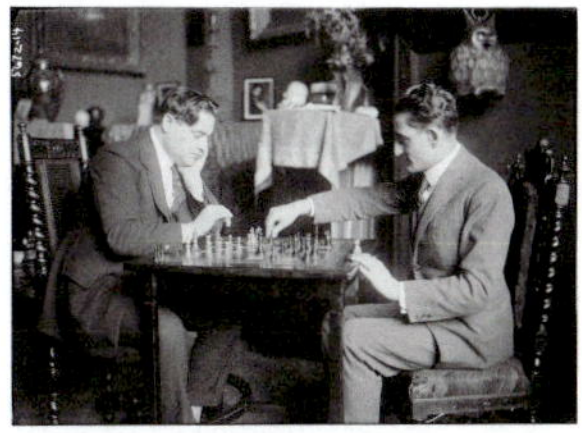

066

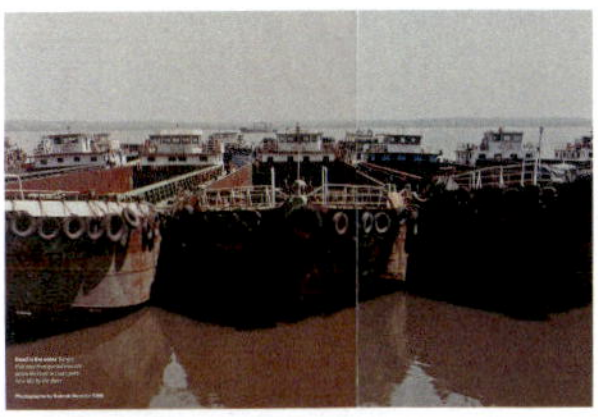

067

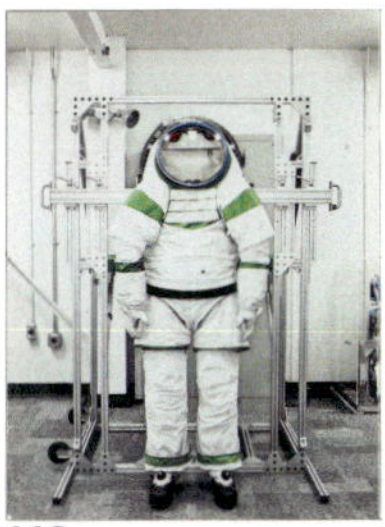

068

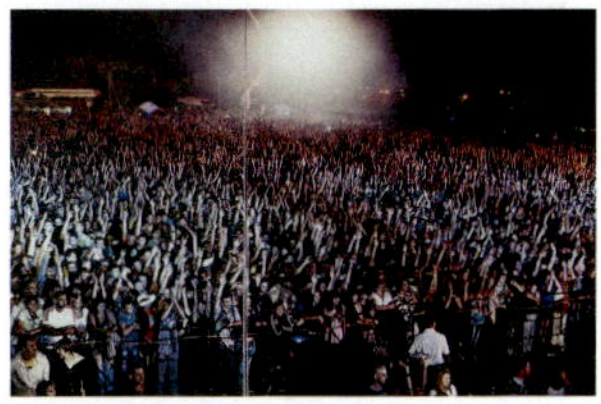

069

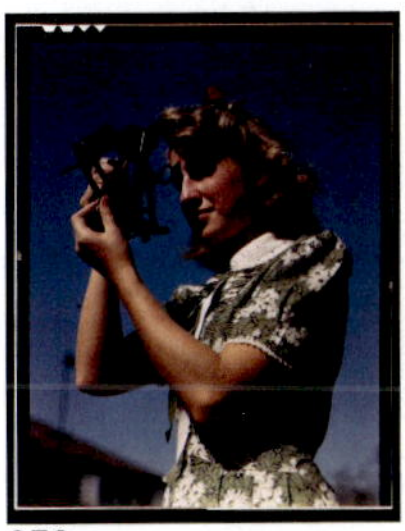

070

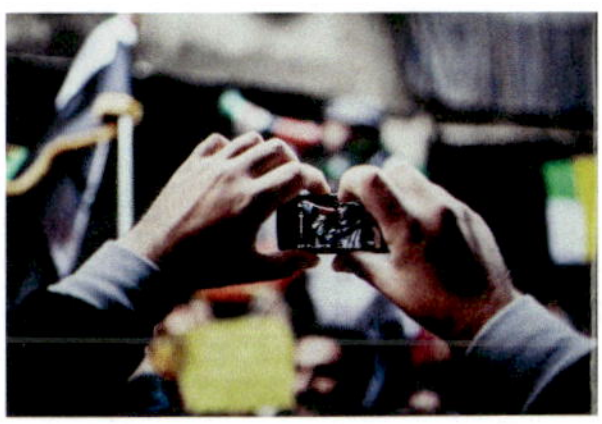

071

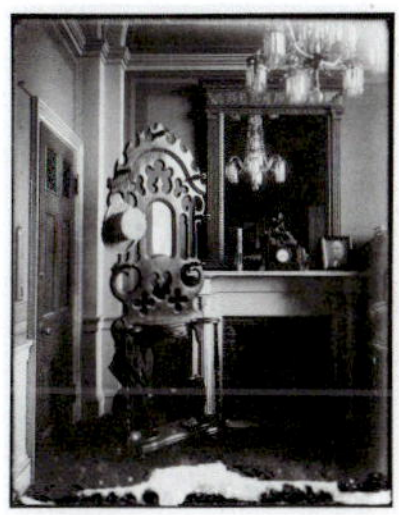

072

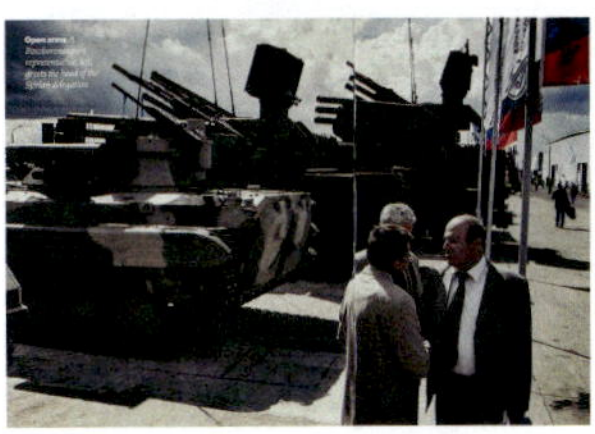

073

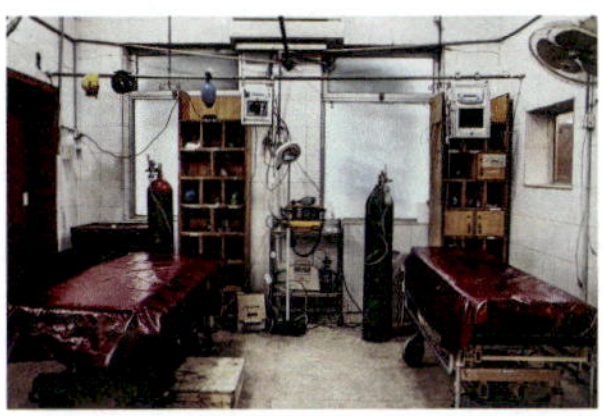

074

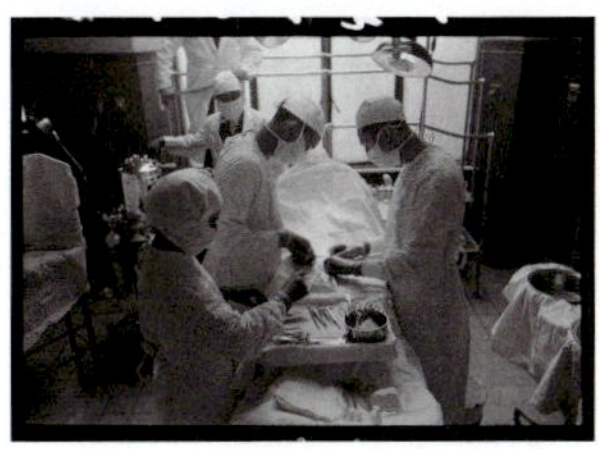

075

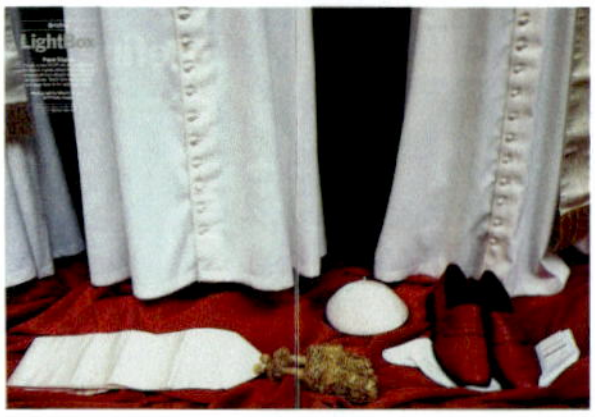

076

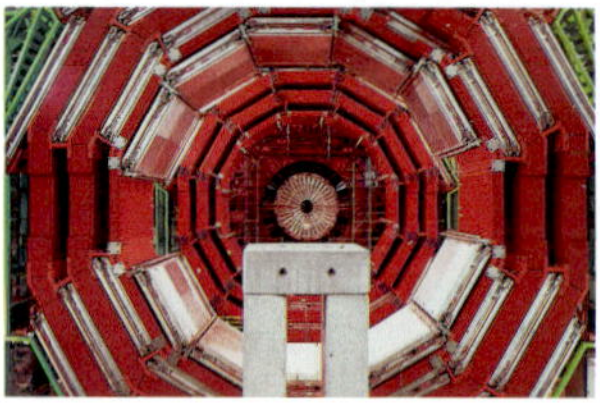

077

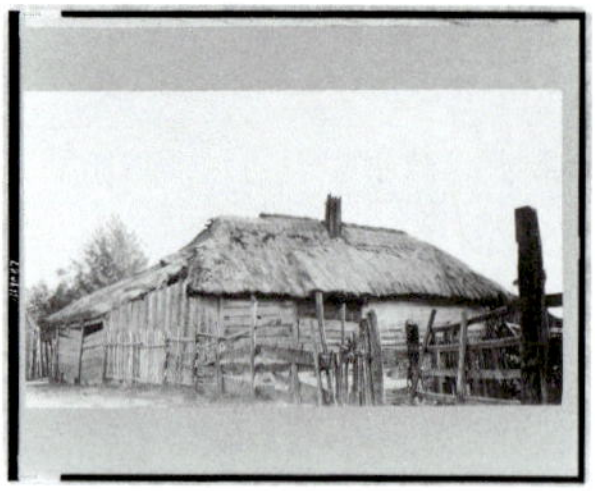

078

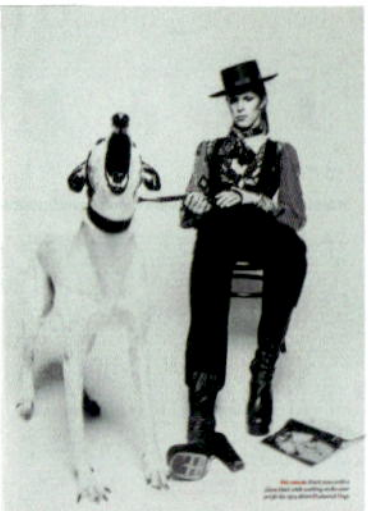

079

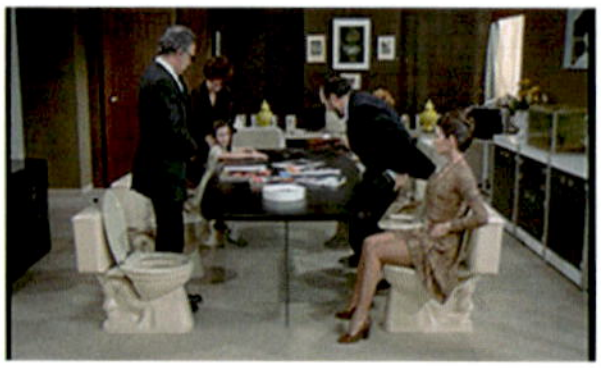

080

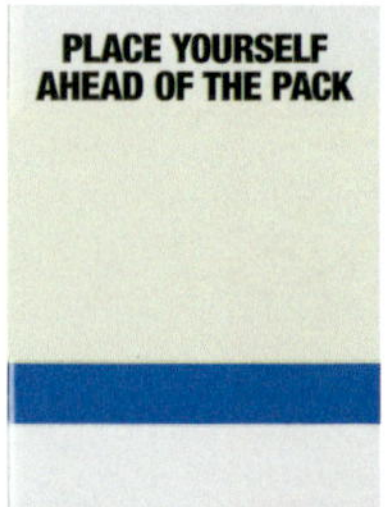

081

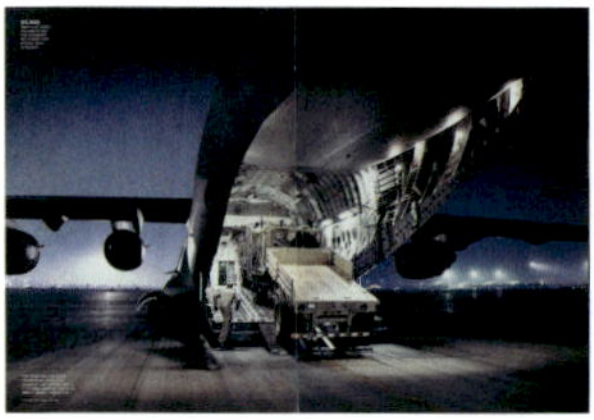

082

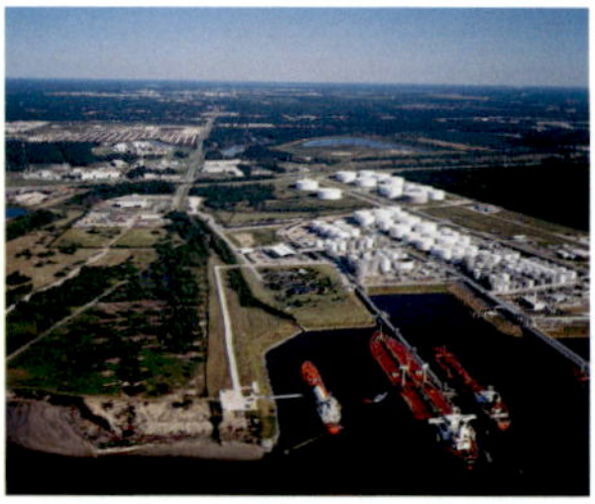

083

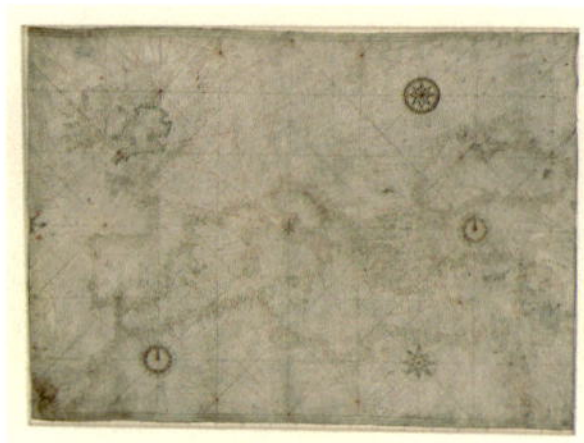

084

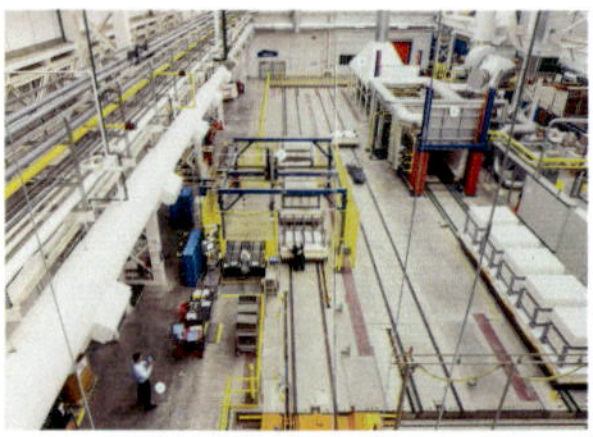

085

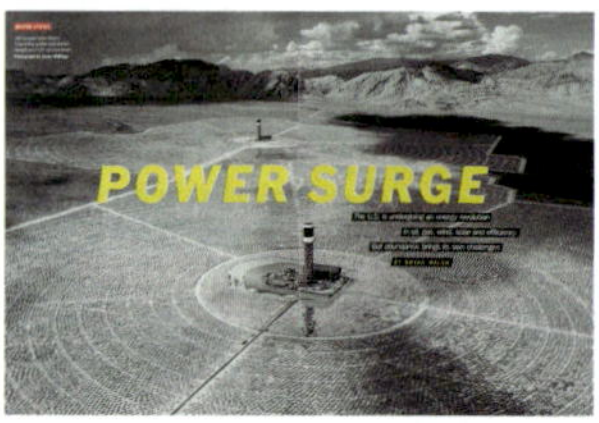

086

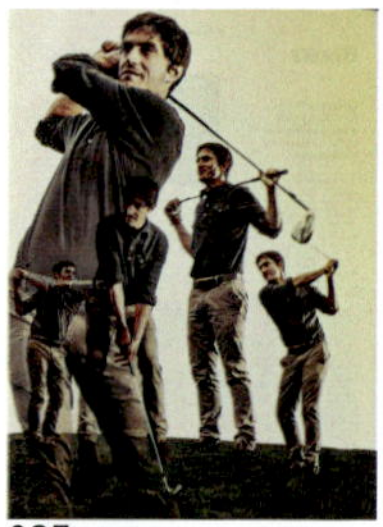

087

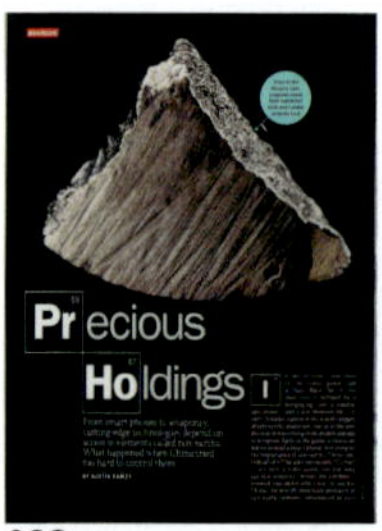

088

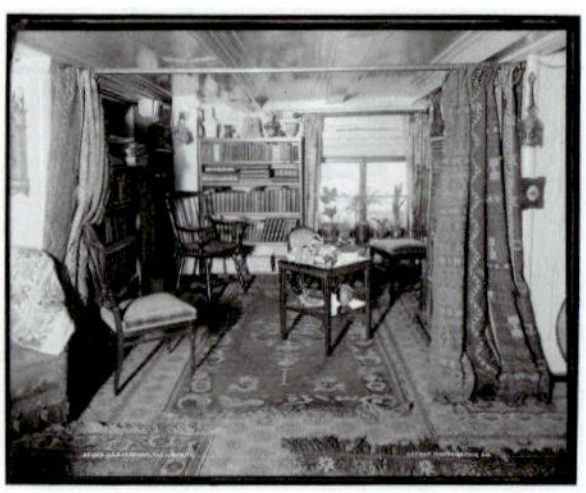

089

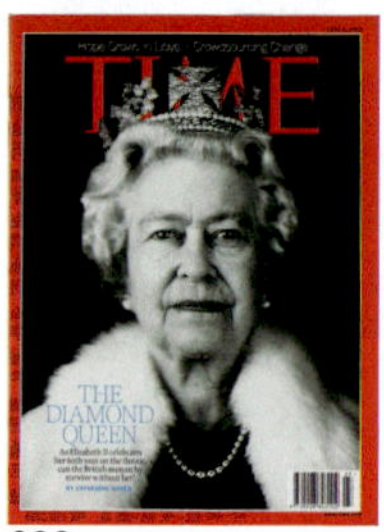

090

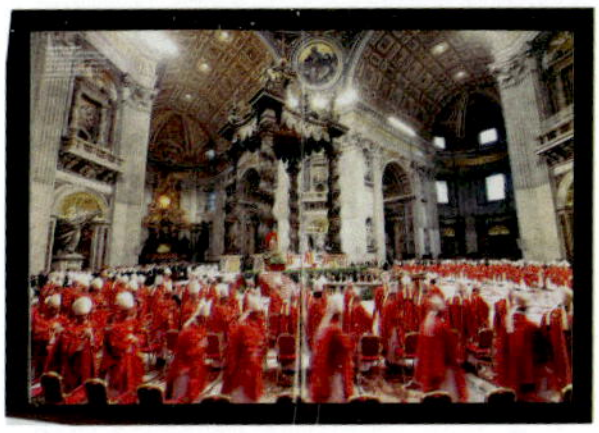

091

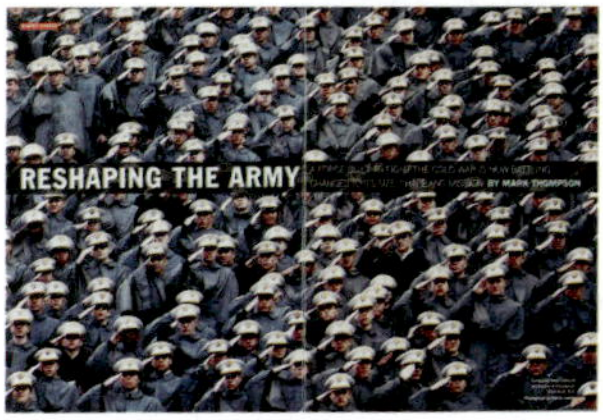

092

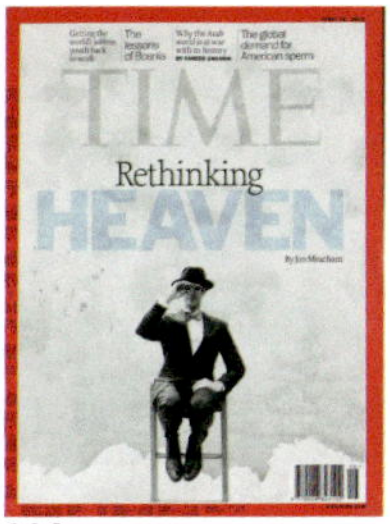

093

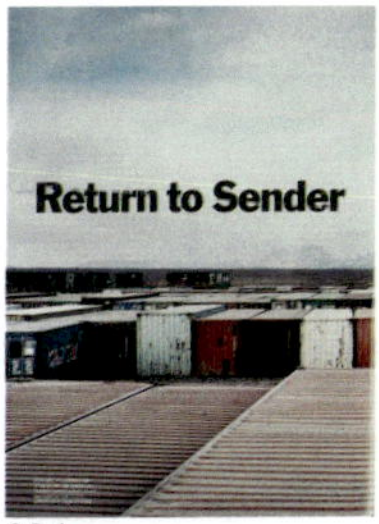

094

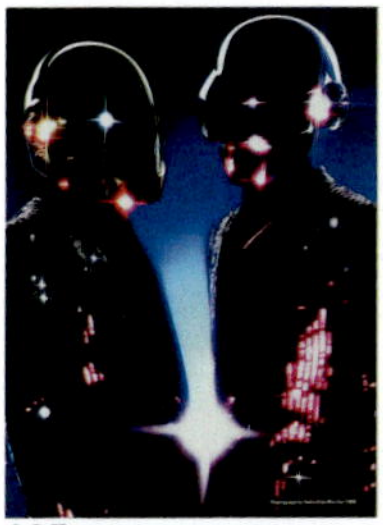

095

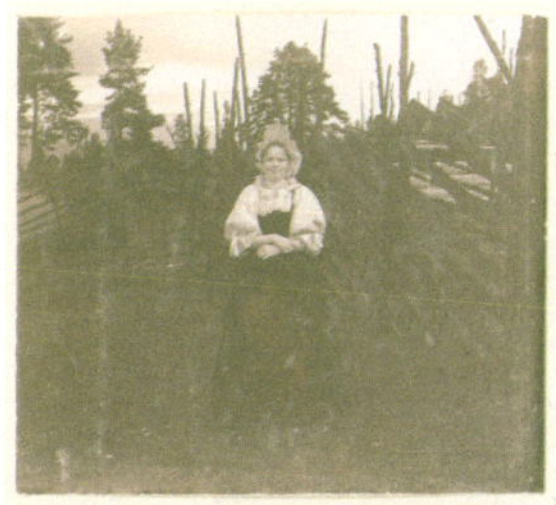

096

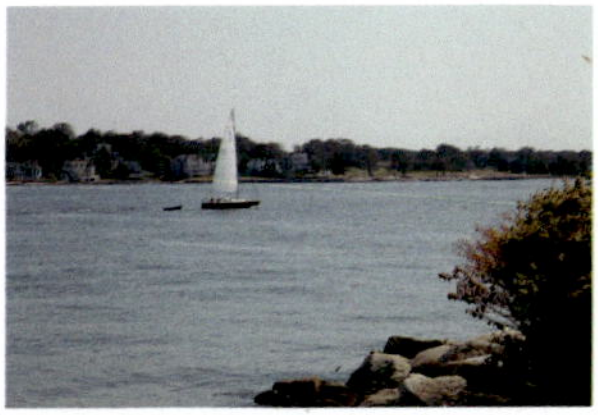

097

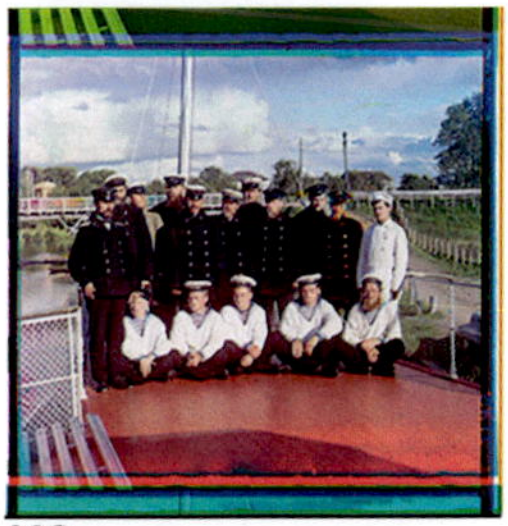

098

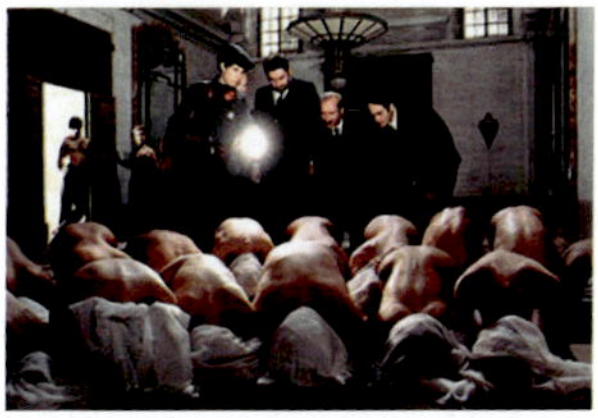

099

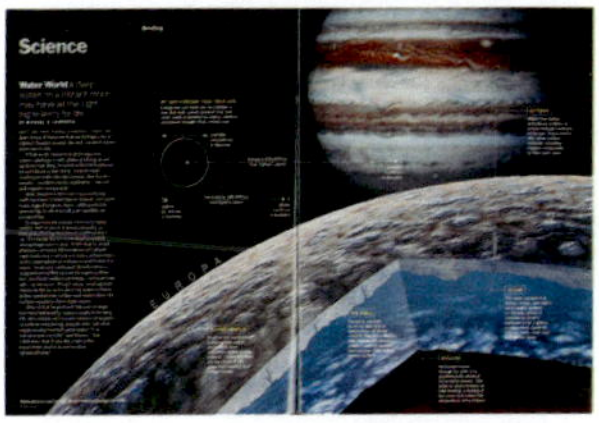

100

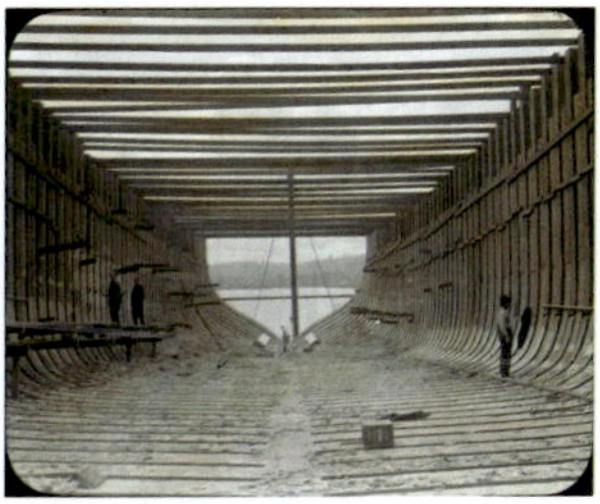

101

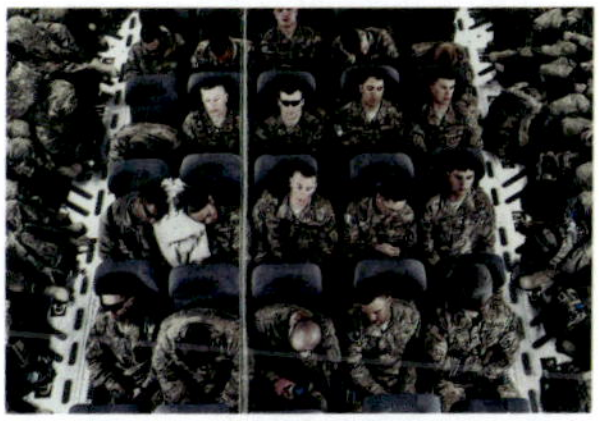

102

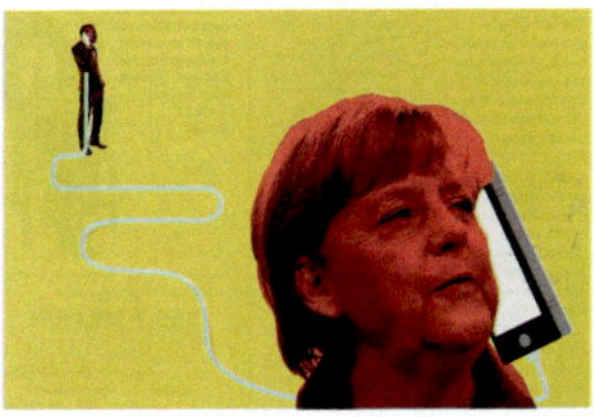

103

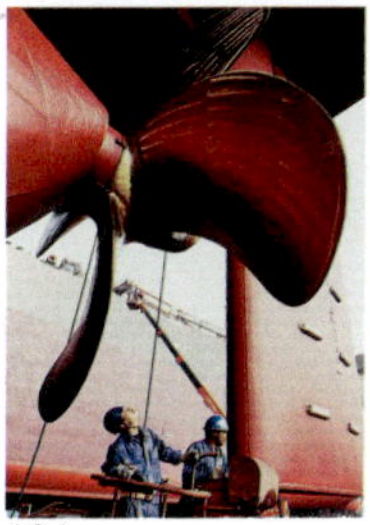

104

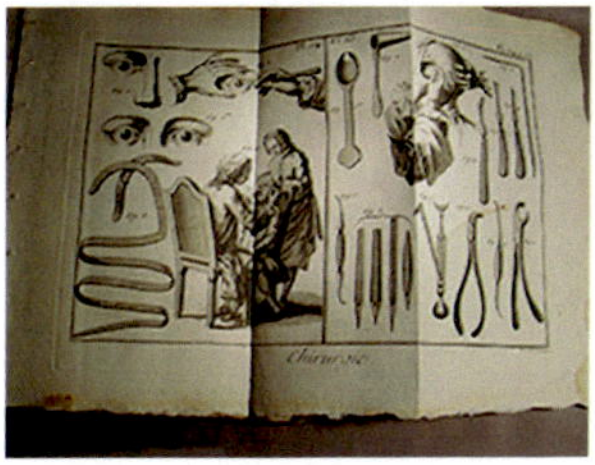

105

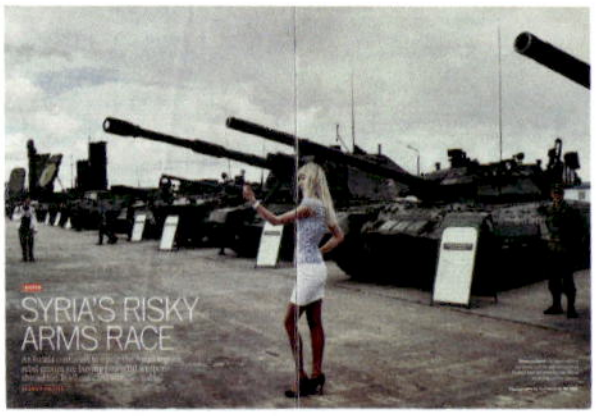

106

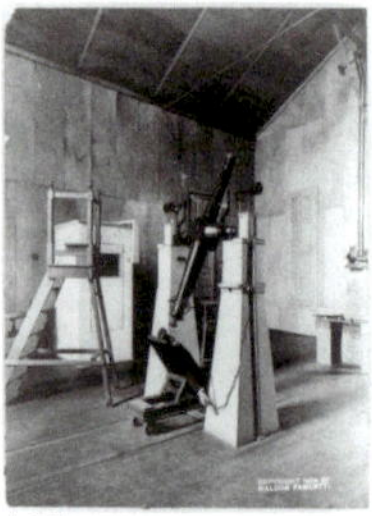

107

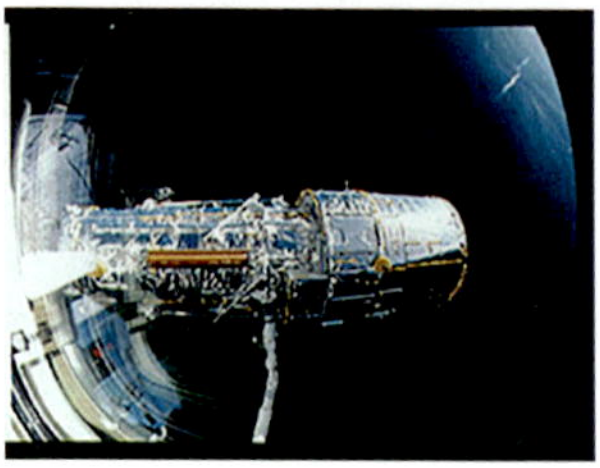

108

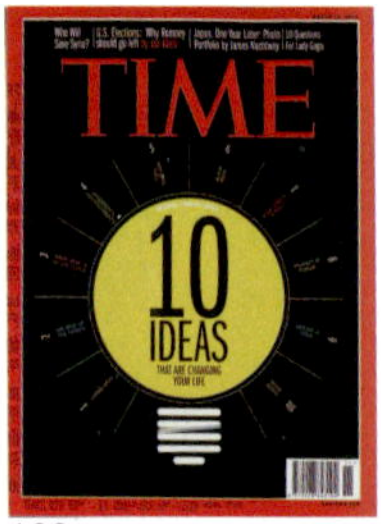

109

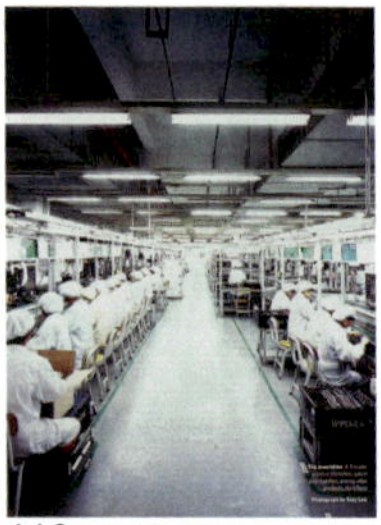

110

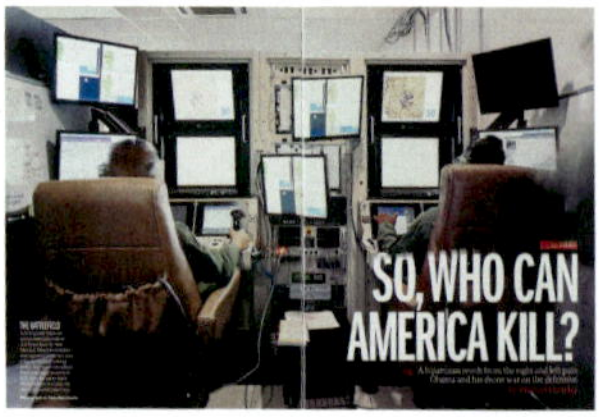

111

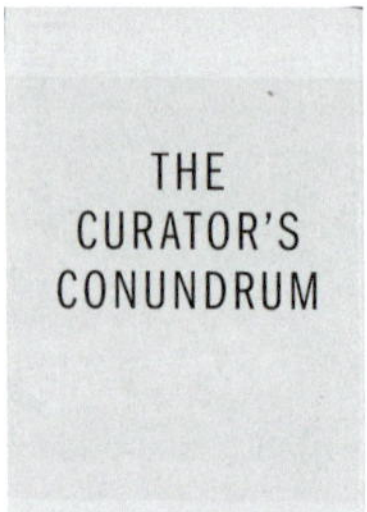

112

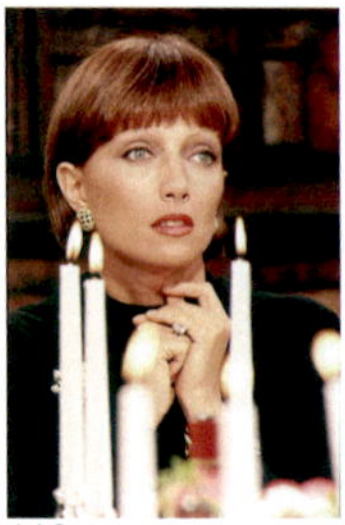

113

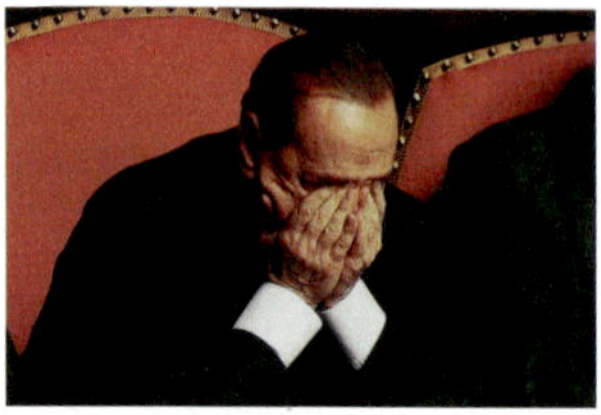

114

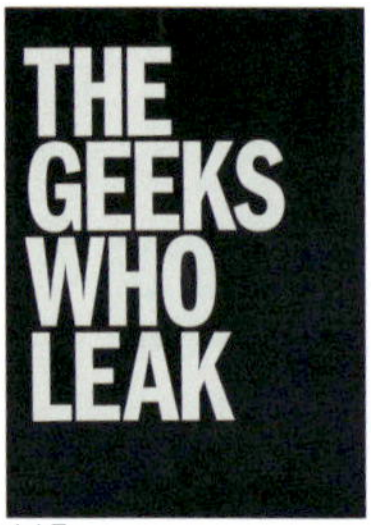

115

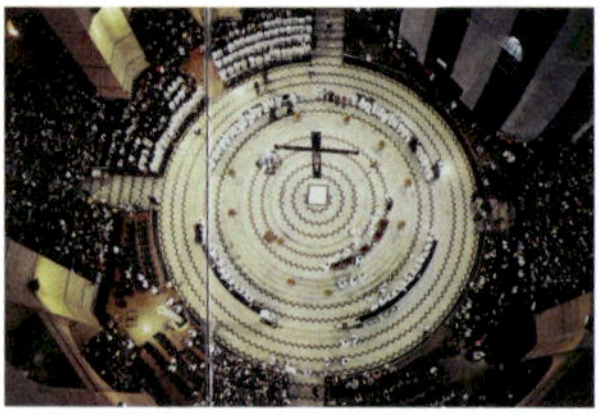

116

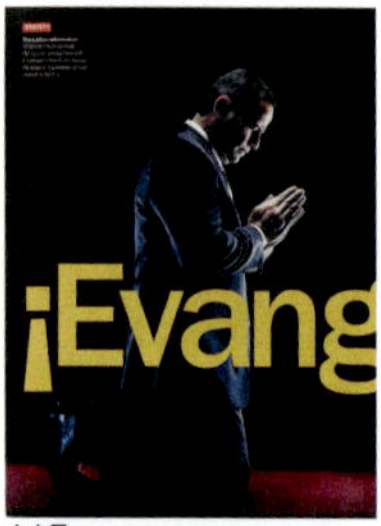

117

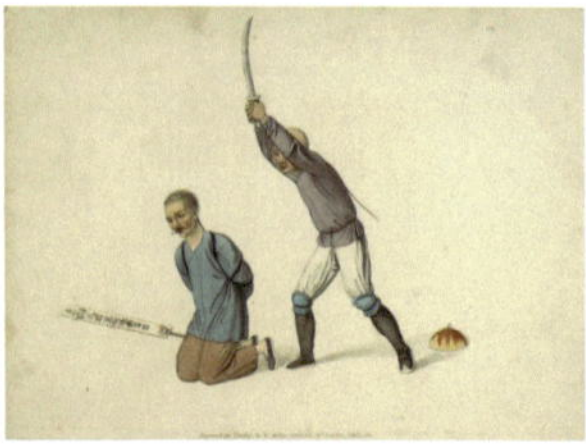

118

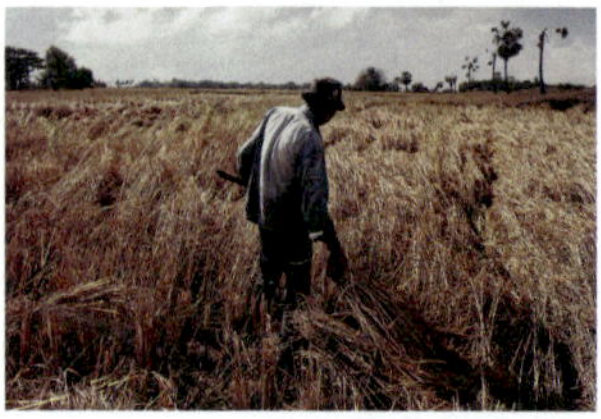

119

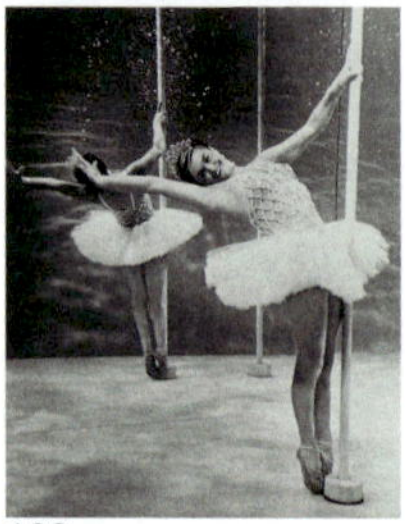

120

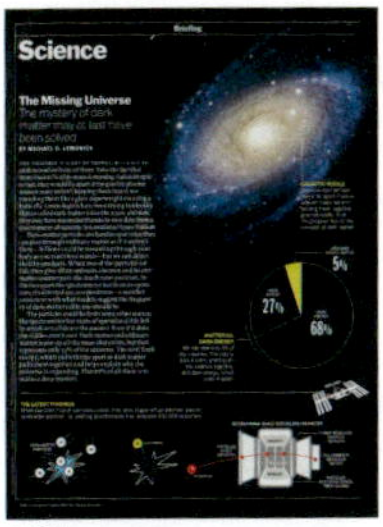

121

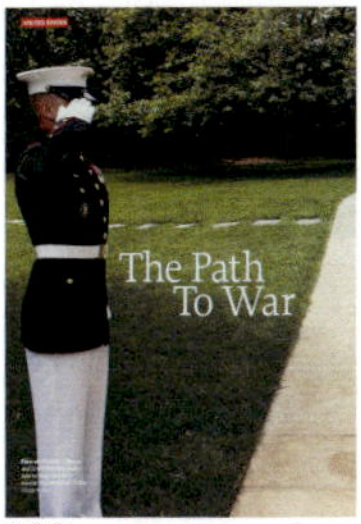

122

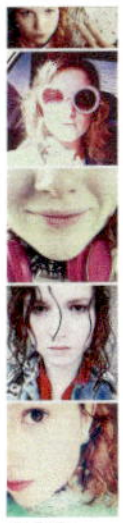

123

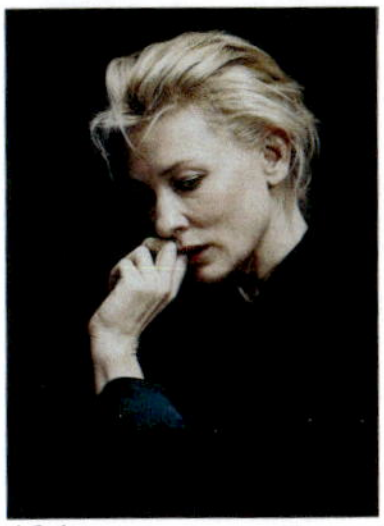

124

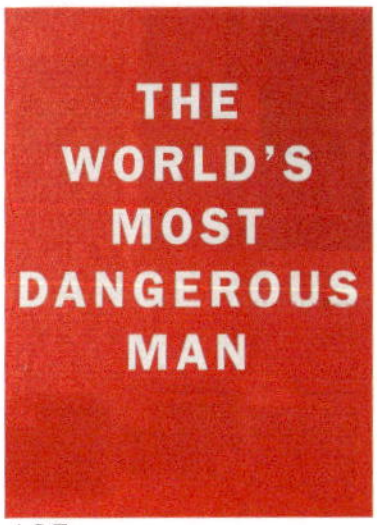

125

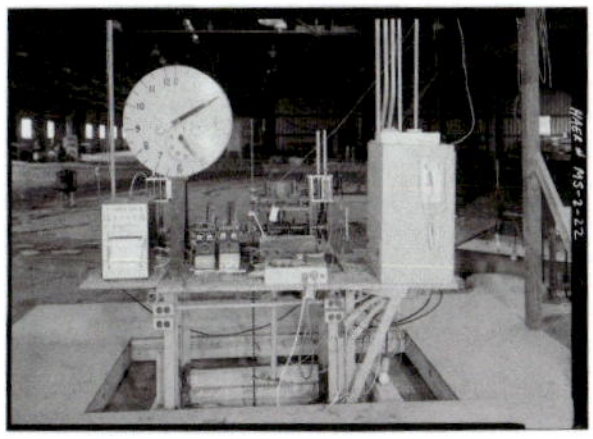

126

127

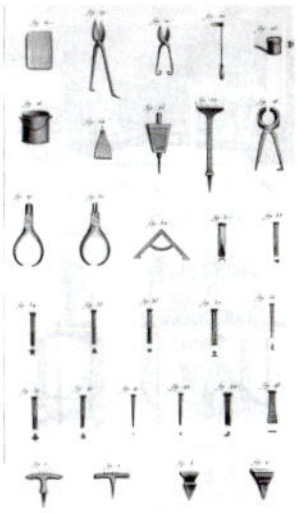

128

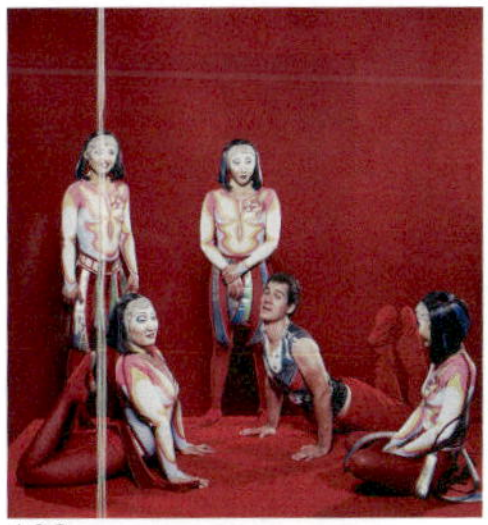

129

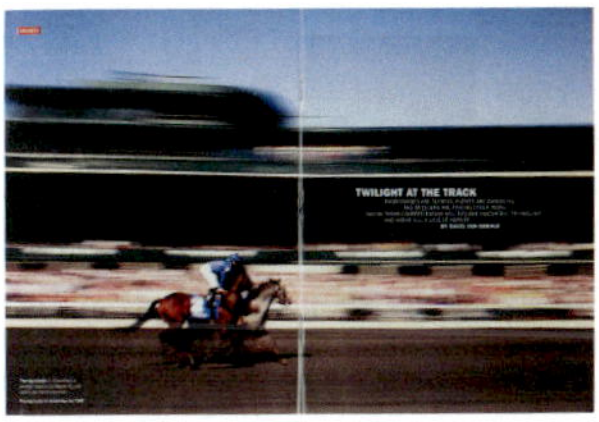

130

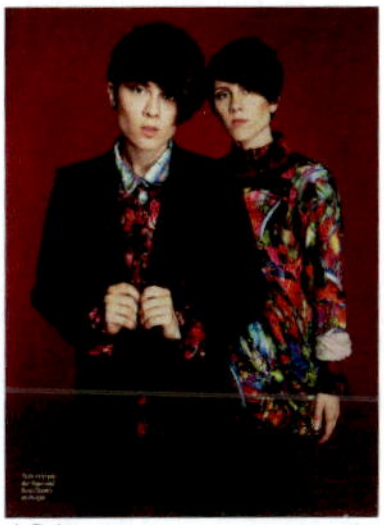

131

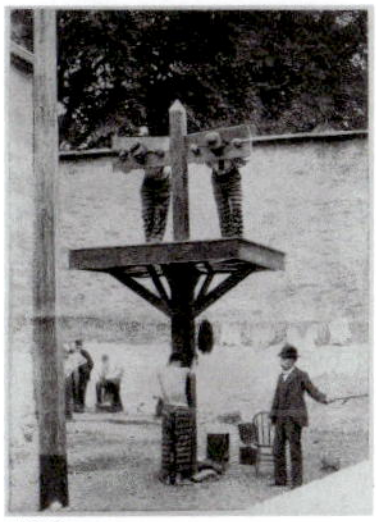

132

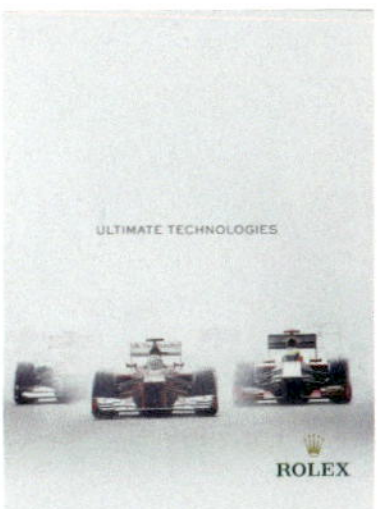

133

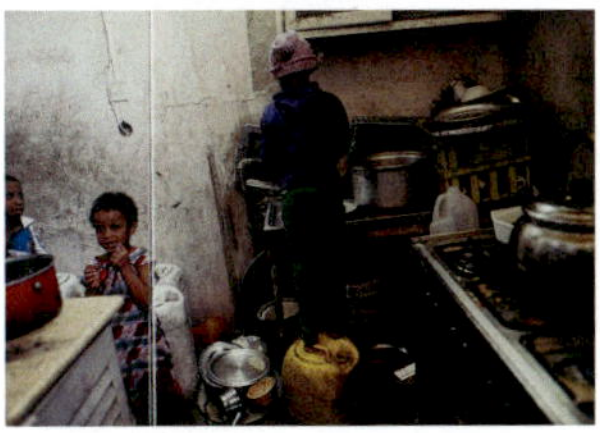

134

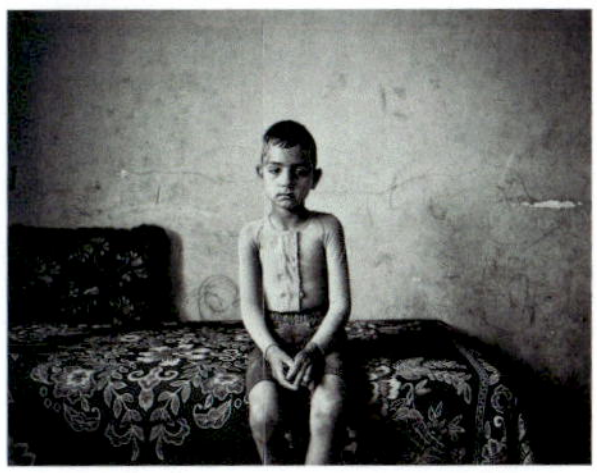

135

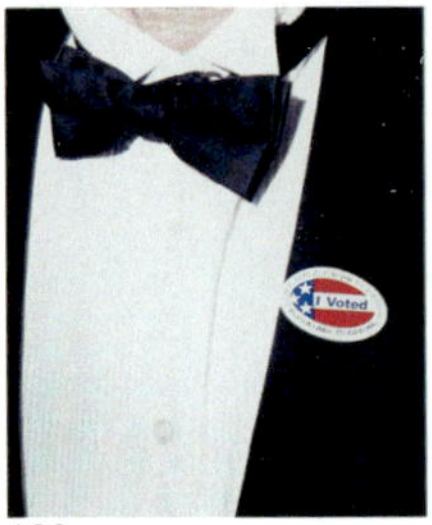

136

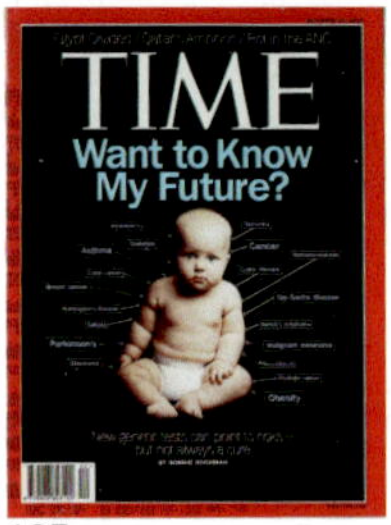

137

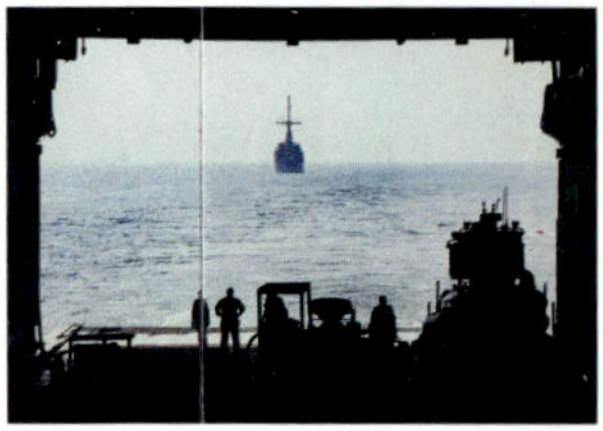

138

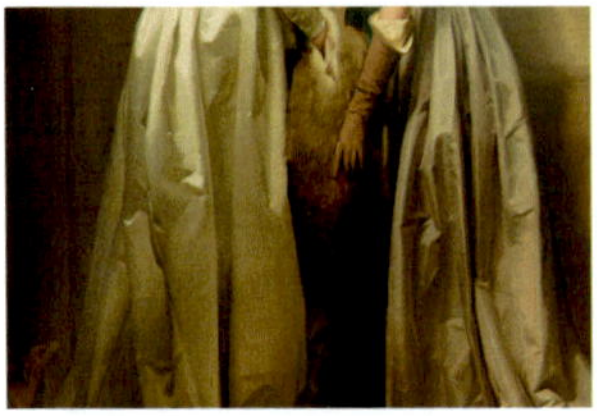

139

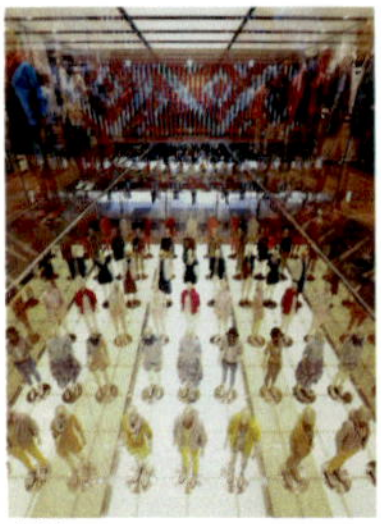

140

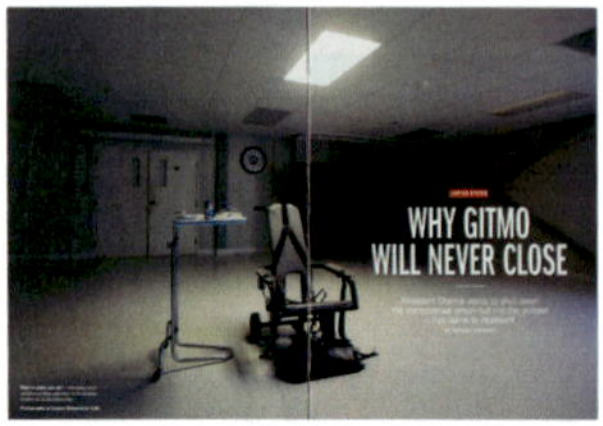

141

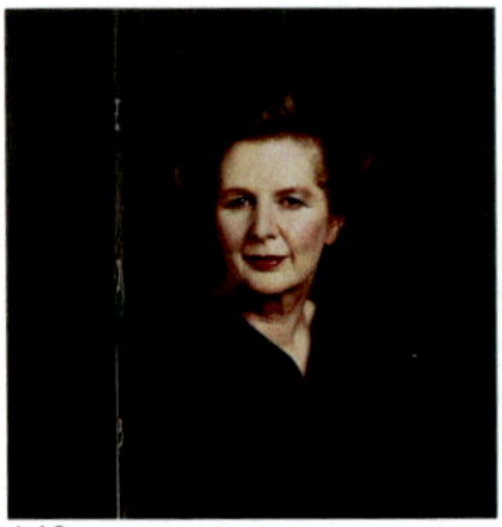

142

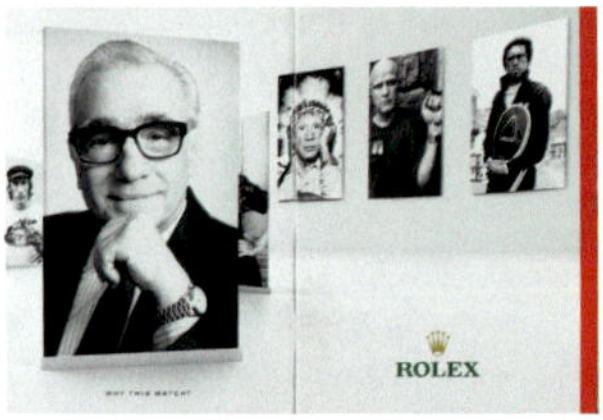

143

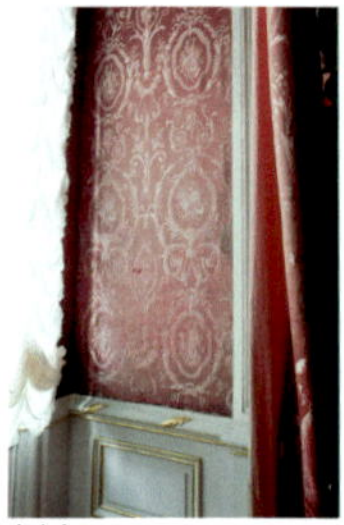

144

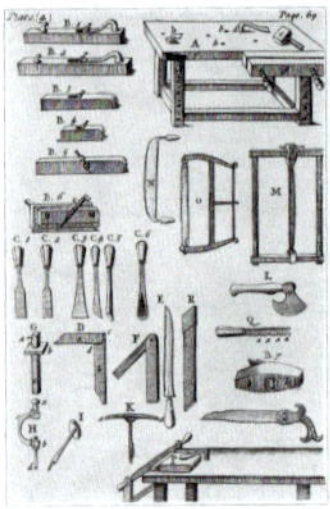

145

ALPHABETIC LIST OF IMAGE TITLES

001. A man of sincere faith
002. A place in the pulpit
003. A quiet revolution
004. Agriculture
005. Architecture
006. Armies
007. Artillery
008. Astrolabe
009. Beard
010. Berlin
011. Billiards
012. Black sea
013. Blind faith
014. Books
015. Boston museum of fine arts
016. Botanical gardens
017. Bvlgari
018. Cabbage soup
019. Cabbage
020. Carpentry
021. Carruth's first film
022. Cathedral of science
023. Charles x, carriage, Versailles, France
024. Chemistry
025. Church
026. Colonialism
027. Confidence woman
028. Crossing over
029. Dancing
030. Dassault systems
031. David Bowie
032. Diderot encyclopedia
033. Dissecting bodies
034. Earth's evolution
035. Eating
036. Elegance is an attitude
037. Face time
038. Fitzsimon's general hospital, Chapel
039. Five ideas
040. Floor plan of observatory
041. Games
042. Garden
043. Golden boy
044. Griffith observatory LA
045. Houston at Newark
046. How to cure cancer
047. Human anatomy
048. I would like to give a blessing
049. In every woman is a queen
050. Inside an observatory
051. Inside Putin's Russia
052. King in the park
053. Lake
054. Last year at Marienbad
055. Li Na
056. Longines
057. Made in china
058. Magic cicadas in the mood
059. Magnus Carlsen
060. Man laying on platform with head in wooden collar
061. Man who would save Europe
062. Marble carving
063. Marie Antoinette
064. Mars
065. Mathematical instruments
066. Men playing chess
067. Metal fatigue
068. NASA space suit
069. National pride
070. Navigation
071. New weapon of war
072. Old hat
073. Open arms
074. Operating theatre Saidu Sharif hospital
075. Operation
076. Papal staples
077. Particle accelerator
078. Peasant's house
079. Pet sounds
080. Phantom of liberty
081. Place yourself ahead of the pack
082. Port dogs

083. Port of Houston Texas
084. Portolan chart of the Mediterranean, the Black Sea, and the coasts of Europe and northwest Africa
085. Power plant
086. Power surge
087. Practice makes perfect
088. Precious holdings
089. Private library
090. Queen Elizabeth
091. Religion
092. Reshaping the army
093. Rethinking heaven
094. Return to sender
095. Robots rebooted
096. Russian peasant
097. Sailing in Connecticut on the long island sound
098. Sailors
099. Salò or the 120 days of Sodom
100. Science
101. Ship building
102. Soldiers from the 101st airborne division
103. Spy vs spy
104. Staying afloat
105. Surgery
106. Syria's risky arms race
107. Telescope of naval observatory
108. Telescope
109. Ten ideas
110. The assembler
111. The battlefield
112. The discrete charm of the bourgeoisie
113. The curator's conundrum
114. The face of defeat
115. The geeks who leak
116. The Latin American challenge
117. The Latino reformation
118. The manner of beheading
119. The marginalized
120. The mermaid of MGM musicals
121. The missing universe
122. The path to war
123. The photographer
124. The queen stands alone
125. The world's most dangerous man
126. Tide generator
127. To catch a thief
128. Tools
129. Trapeze
130. Twilight at the track
131. Twin sister pop
132. Two prisoners in pillory with another tied to whipping post below and a man with whip
133. Ultimate technologies
134. Underclass
135. Victim's face
136. VIP ballot
137. Want to know my future?
138. War games
139. Wealth
140. What's in store
141. Why Gimto will never close
142. Why the iron lady endures
143. Why this watch
144. Window
145. Wood working tools

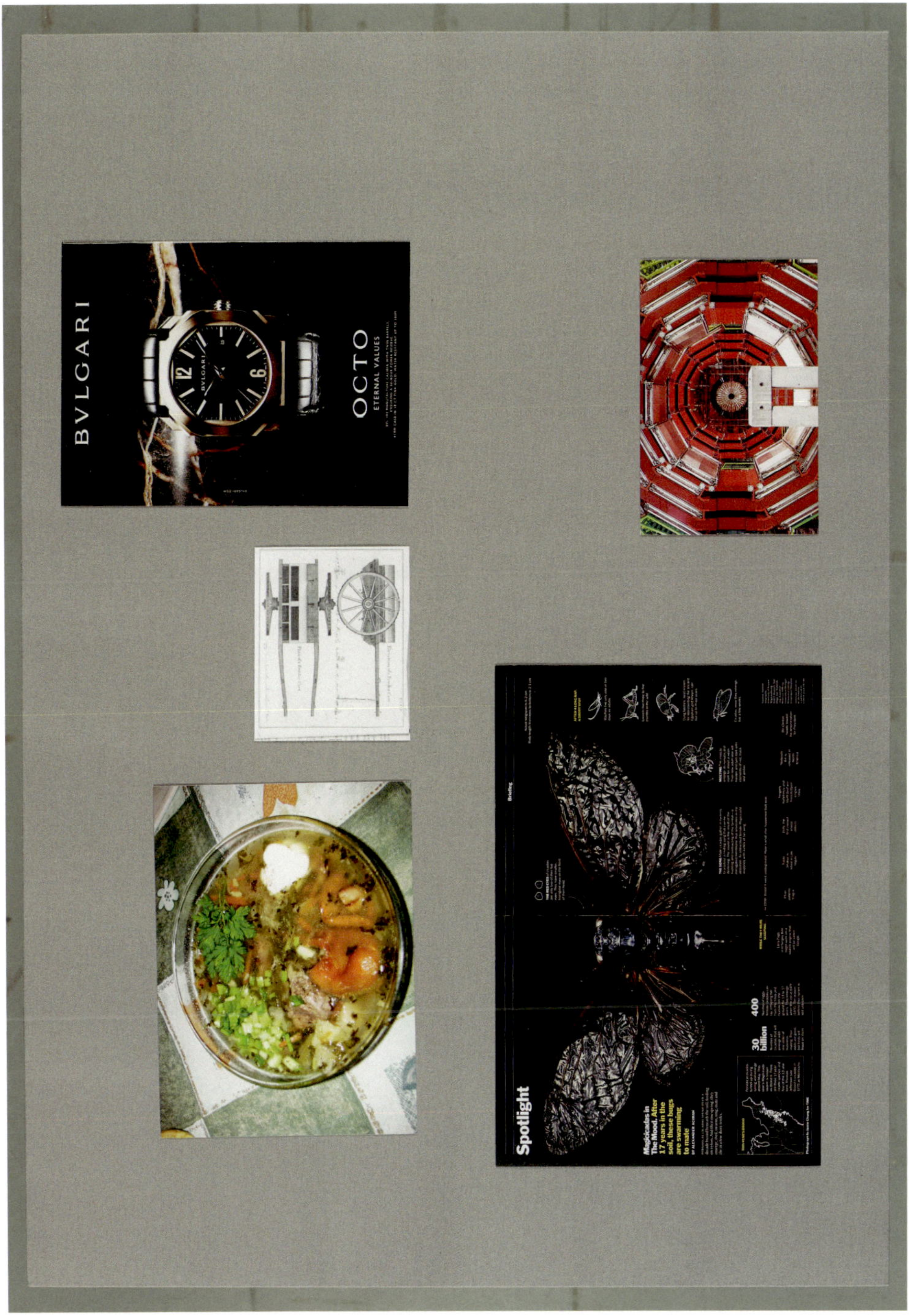

aerial view (plate 3) MA

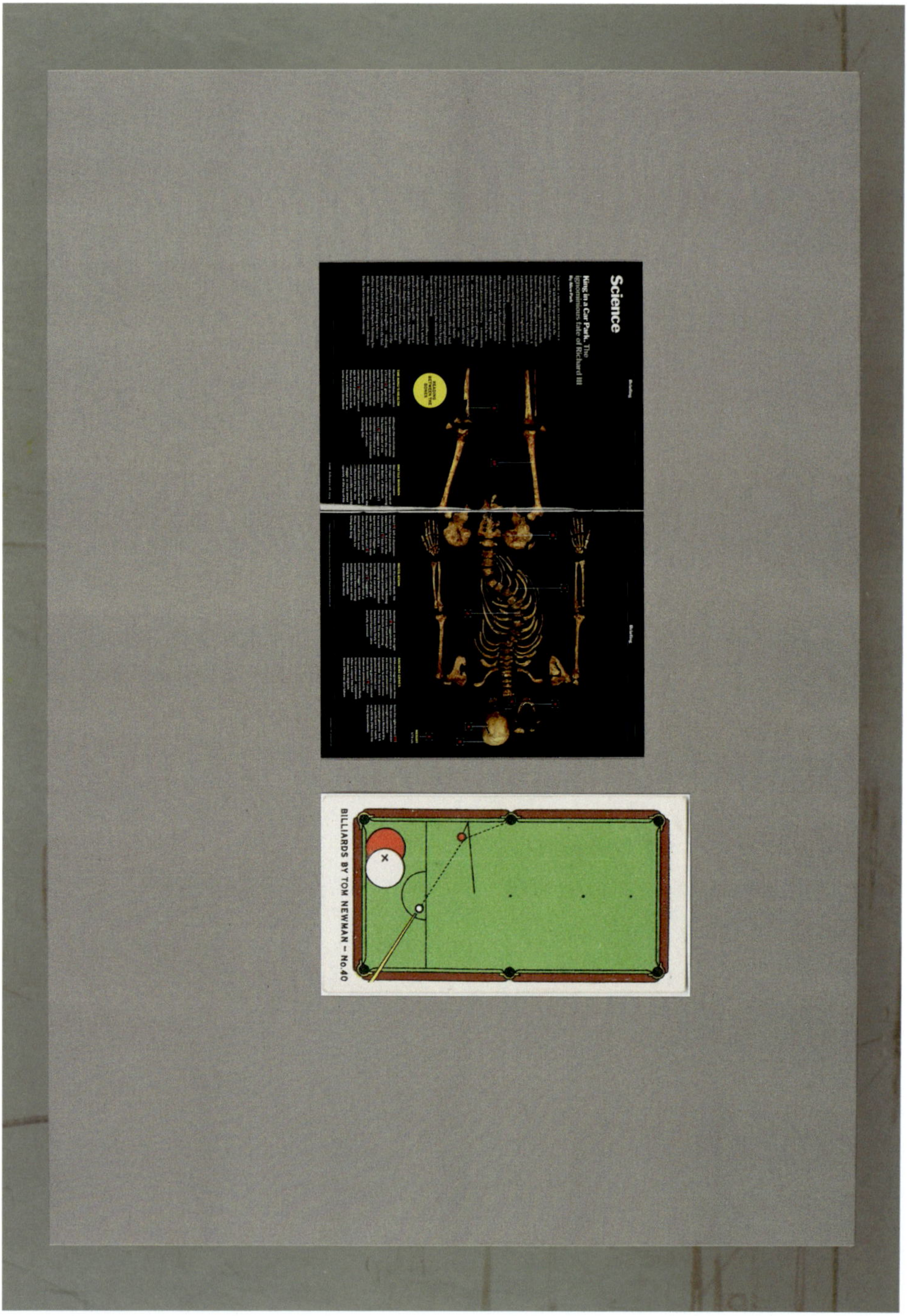

aerial view (plate 5) MA

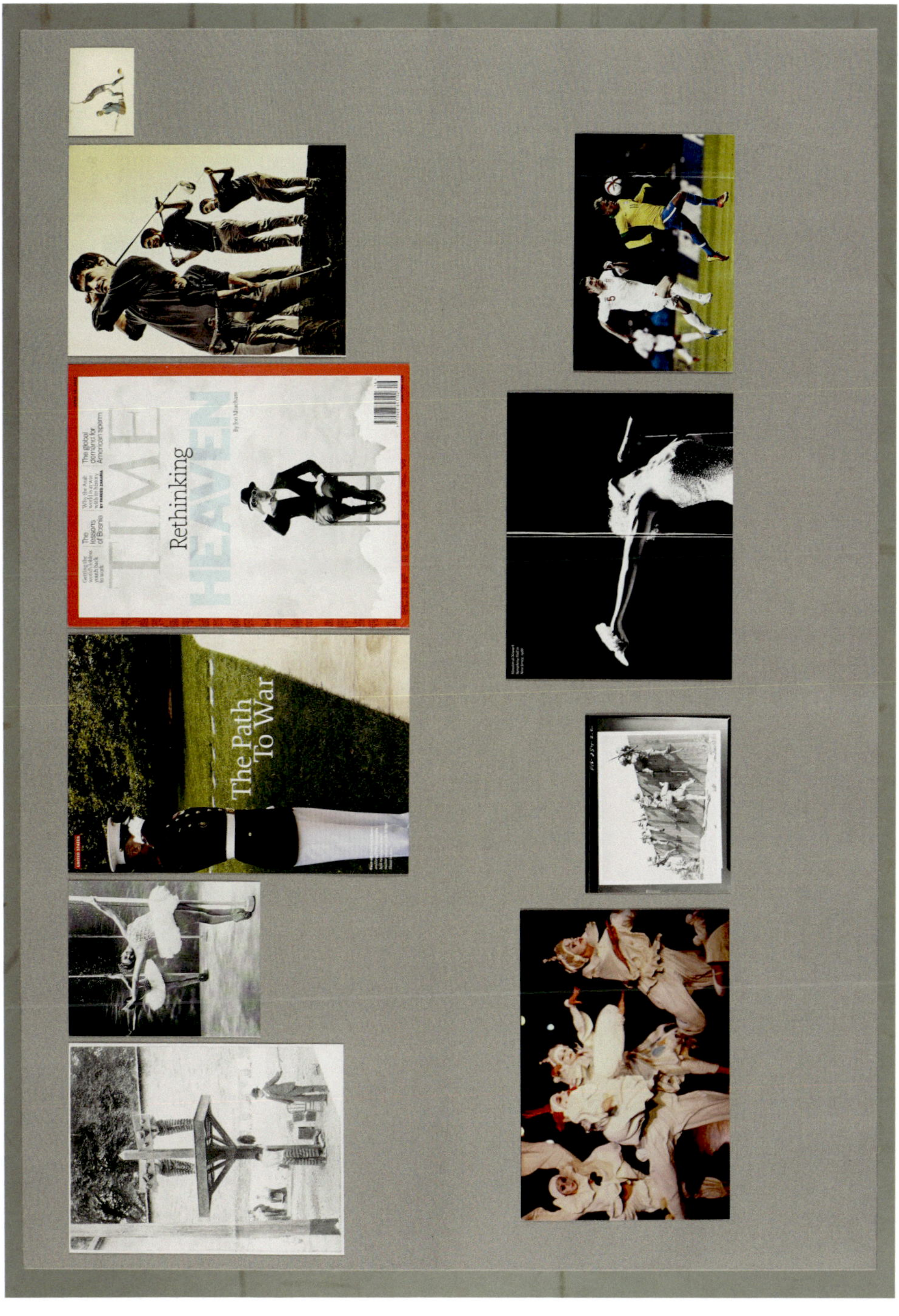

arms raised (plate 1) MA

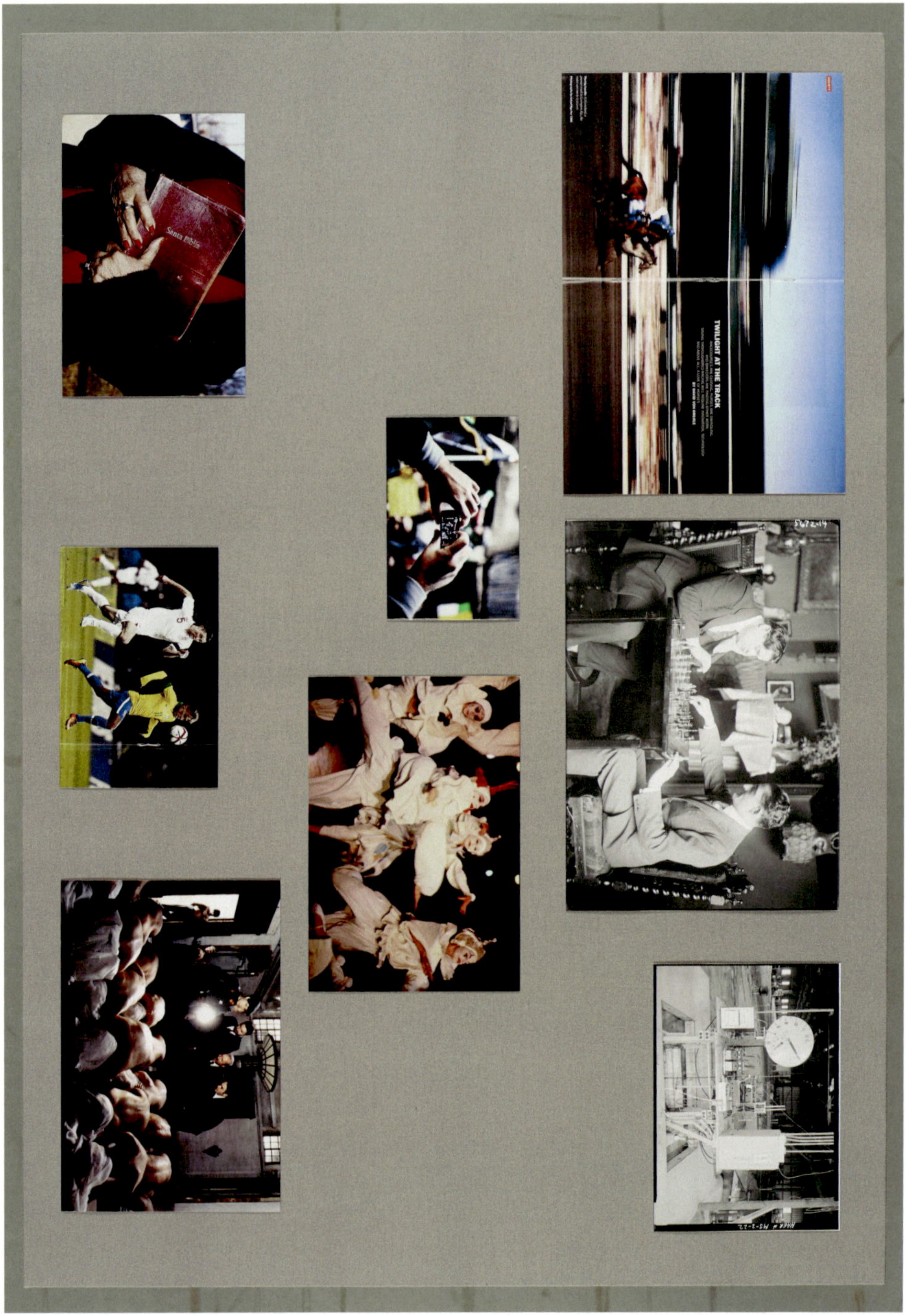

Joseph Grigely

READING RECTANGLES

The question, as I see it, is about how we read rectangles: typically photographs, either as individual images or as arrays of images that populate historical and contemporary media. Their legibility is generally not a point of dispute, especially the legibility of images that can be identified in a referential way: there are people, there are animals, there are objects, and so on. But how we move beyond legibility to readability — to identify meaning within the rectangles, to relate the content of one rectangle to another, and to map or otherwise organize the rectangles according to some taxonomic scheme — those are different tasks altogether, and fundamental to how we read the endless spread of images that constitutes our daily experience of seeing.

It all starts with the images themselves — with the 'collection' of a body of visual information. The material objects and images that comprise human knowledge come to us in different ways: collections, archives, assemblages, and the accumulations of expeditions to lands and to libraries. They range from collections encompassing both art and natural history, like Rudolph II's *Wunderkammer*, to hoards of unnatural history, like the Collyer brothers' apartment in New York, where their unimaginable piles of the detritus of daily living towered to the ceilings and buried their own bodies after they died. It is possible to imagine a map of Rudolph's collection; but a map of the layered and compressed information in the apartment at 2078 Fifth Avenue almost defies the imagination: the combined weight of the newspapers, magazines, books, and chattels they had accumulated was estimated to be 140 tons, or 127,006 kilograms. Likewise, the daily production of images on Instagram or Facebook is almost beyond human comprehension — we could with some effort create a collection of images produced over a period of 24 hours — but how would we organize it outside of the chronology that produced it?

Collecting, accumulating, hoarding, and archiving are not necessarily the same sort of activities. Collecting involves something deliberate and willed, even if one isn't sure how the discrete parts all come together. The sense in which we use the English word 'collection' to reference objects of interest — scientific specimens and artworks, for example — began in England in the 17th century when the diarist John Evelyn wrote about visiting Pierre Morine in Paris in 1651. Morine, observed Evelyn, "had abundance of incomparable shells, at least 1000 sorts, which furnish'd a Cabinet of greate price, & a very curious collection of Scarabies & insects, of which he was compiling a natural historie."[1] This observation is an important one. What distinguishes a collection from an accumulation is a sense of modulated purpose. Behind every collection is desire. An archive can make no comparable claim. An archive is arbitrary, for it consists of material too important as history to throw away, and too unimportant as cultural documents to disseminate among the public. A collection is often symmetrical, initially shaping itself from the possibilities within an accumulation, like the quotations that make up Benjamin's *Arcades Project*, or the photographs that accumulate to constitute a portrait in the work of Hans Peter Feldmann. The shape might derive from prescribed parameters that define the borders of the collection, however permeable they might actually be. In an exhibition catalogue that accompanied Alexis Rockman's exhibition at Jay Gorney Modern Art in 1992, Douglas Blau compiled an alphabetical 'index' to Rockman's exhibition — using the index as an organizational tool to delineate the means by which we catalogue the biological world. The words that appear most frequently in Blau's index are words that reflect on our desire for empirical knowledge by assembling bits and pieces of the world in a single place: within, for example, an encyclopedia, a museum, a curiosity cabinet, or even an attic. Blau's index does not include the word 'archive', but it does include the word 'collection', like this:

> *Collection: as catalogue, 29, 255, 410-412, 415-422, 441-448, 466, 481, 739; as closed and/or open set, 62-63, 403, 415-416; as compilation, 255, 404-409, 426; as depository, 422, 450, 467-469, 552; exclusion and inclusion in selection of, 63, 402-404, 407, 487, 543; inventories of, 452, 468; as lexicon, 48, 420-422, 426; as list, 69, 415; presentation of specimen in, 408-412, 472, 512, 529, 551-553; preservation and, 421, 720-722; private, 241, 255-256, 317, 401, 467, 552; public, 423, 449-451, 535-537, 570; as recollection, 6-8; still life as, 452-459, 461; taxonomy and, 1-6, 255, 442-428, 545-556; variety and singularity in, 97, 462-469, 481*[2]

Blau's *Index* reminds us that a collection without an index is merely an array. The collection may have been deliberately arranged, it may have been arbitrarily arranged, or sometimes (as in the case of Sir John Soane's collection of architectural ruins and fragments) the collection is arranged and rearranged according to changing intentions. Soane's collection is devoid of wall labels: walking through the museum is like reading an old magazine where all of the captions have been removed from the pictures. But the sense of order is not entirely absent: Soane ultimately published three "Guides" to his collection (in 1830, 1832, and 1835), each one narrating a different path through it.

Moving through the space of human culture has always been a challenge, as it has always been a challenge to move through any human space and map it. Georges Perec (in *Species of Space*) and Dennis Wood and Robert Beck (in *Home Rules*) have shown us how the maps we create for domestic space have a certain subjectivity that is only partly determined by the space itself. It's a way of saying that our efforts to map human knowledge are also driven by our own inescapable subjectivity. In the 3rd century B.C., in *The Nature of the Universe*, Lucretius makes a heroic effort to organize the space of life under and around the sun: matter and space, movement and atoms, life and mind, sensation and sex, cosmology, sociology, meteorology and geology. In *The Elizabethan World Picture*, E.M. W. Tillyard attempted to present a Renaissance cosmology that was a Chain of Being occupied by God, angels, humans, animals, vegetables, and minerals. With Diderot's *Encyclopedia*, the shape of the universe became increasingly understood as having rational order — where the sciences, mathematics, medicine, philosophy, political theory, and the arts were organized not according to a theocratic relationship, but a humanistic one.

With Aby Warburg's *Mnemosyne Atlas*, which the art historian started in 1924 and left unfinished at his death in 1929, we enter a new period in the history of studying human knowledge, one that focuses on rhetorical strategies of visual information design. The Mnemosyne Atlas is relevant as a critical apparatus, as a visual display, and as an exercise in proximal relations. As a visual apparatus it distinguishes itself from previous efforts to map knowledge by using images, or representations of art, rather than the art itself. Where the biological *wunderkammer* contains mounted specimens from nature, Warburg's Atlas contains 2-dimensional black and white prints, thereby marking a turn from the real to its representation.

Warburg's *Mnemosyne Atlas* consists of sixty three wood panels covered with black cloth. Onto these panels Warburg arranged a number of images, affixed to the panels and to each other using pins, thumb tacks, and paper clips. The images seem to query human relations, and the motions of the human body, without explicitly captioning these subjects. The images came from art history, primarily, but also included manuscripts, advertisements, postage stamps, and images from magazines, newspapers, and other forms of contemporary media. Warburg's visual information was skimmed from readily available sources — the critical prestidigitation is in how it is arranged. The panels were then photographed, and the photographs serve as a critical commentary on the arrangements.

Fast forward 90 years to Fari Shams' *European Civilization, Peter the Great, and the Order of Things*, and there is a sense of uncanny recognition. Shams' *Peter the Great* consists of two hundred and twelve panels covered with gray cloth. It is a gray very close to Kodak's "neutral gray". Onto these panels Shams arranged arrays of images. They are not an arbitrary collection of images, but rather images that evince particular traits of the personality of Peter the Great. Like Warburg's images, they come from art history, primarily, but also include manuscripts, advertisements, and images from magazines, newspapers, and other forms of contemporary media. But what is 'contemporary' to Shams was not 'contemporary' to Warburg: where Warburg had newspapers, Shams has the internet, and a superabundance of easily accessible and sourced images. As with Warburg, the critical moment is in the arrangement of the images — which Shams troubles by arranging and rearranging the same images according to different rationales: first in alphabetical order, then taking account of Diderot's taxonomy of knowledge, then Michel Adanson's taxonomy of plants, then the traditional art historian's practice of putting one image beside another, as one page might be said to 'face' another page. The panels were then photographed, and the photographs serve as a critical commentary on the arrangements.

Of course, there are additional differences. Warburg's black panels are 150 x 200cm; Shams' gray panels are 120 x 84 cm. Warburg's panels are typically presented as printed images, usually reduced in scale; Shams' panels are projected onto a wall, enlarging them, but they are also reduced when printed. What remains static is the proportion of the panels.

Bisected vertically in the middle, Shams' panels are the equivalent of an open book, size A0. Warburg's, sometimes presented horizontally, but usually vertically, likewise read as pages in a book. And like pages in a book, they are all sequenced — numbered — albeit, in the case of Warburg's panels, with occasional gaps (9-19 and 65-69 are lacking), indicating their unfinished nature. The primary interpretative challenge largely lies in the trajectory of

our reading of the images in relation to each other. Left to right, top to bottom, each image typically has four sides: four ways into it, four ways out of it. Each image therefore has 16 possible trajectories; as the images add up, two, three, six, ten, twenty six images, the number of reading pathways multiplies exponentially. The possibilities are staggering.

The rectangles are not always perfect Euclidean constructions. Warburg's panels, as photographed in the elliptical library of the Warburg House in Hamburg, reveal behind and around them a context of books and book spines, in effect backgrounding the images in a verbal tangle of history. In this regard they are not totally without critical commentary. The presence of the books, and the way many of the images overlap each other, remind us that images do not come to us in detached from history: this history is always latent, sometimes, as here, hiding in the shadows created by the photographer's lights. The edges of the panels sometimes appear irregular because of the effect of the shadows on the panels: the panels appear less as individual units than they seem to be parts that have broken off from a larger whole. Panel 57 shows this very well: the edges are irregular, what is mathematically rectangular is the frame of the photograph, not the panel itself. The visual arrangement reflects the inherent structure as being discontinuous — fragments pushed up to and into each other, and pushed outward past the edges.

Over a period of years, the *Forschunggruppe Mnemosyne* (based at the gallery 8. Salon in Hamburg) has reconstructed all of Warburg's panels, exhibiting small groups of the panels at various institutions, and with each exhibition developing a critical commentary on the panels. These commentaries include photographs of the reconstructed panels, the individual elements, and maps of possible trajectories of the readings. The reconstructions are not

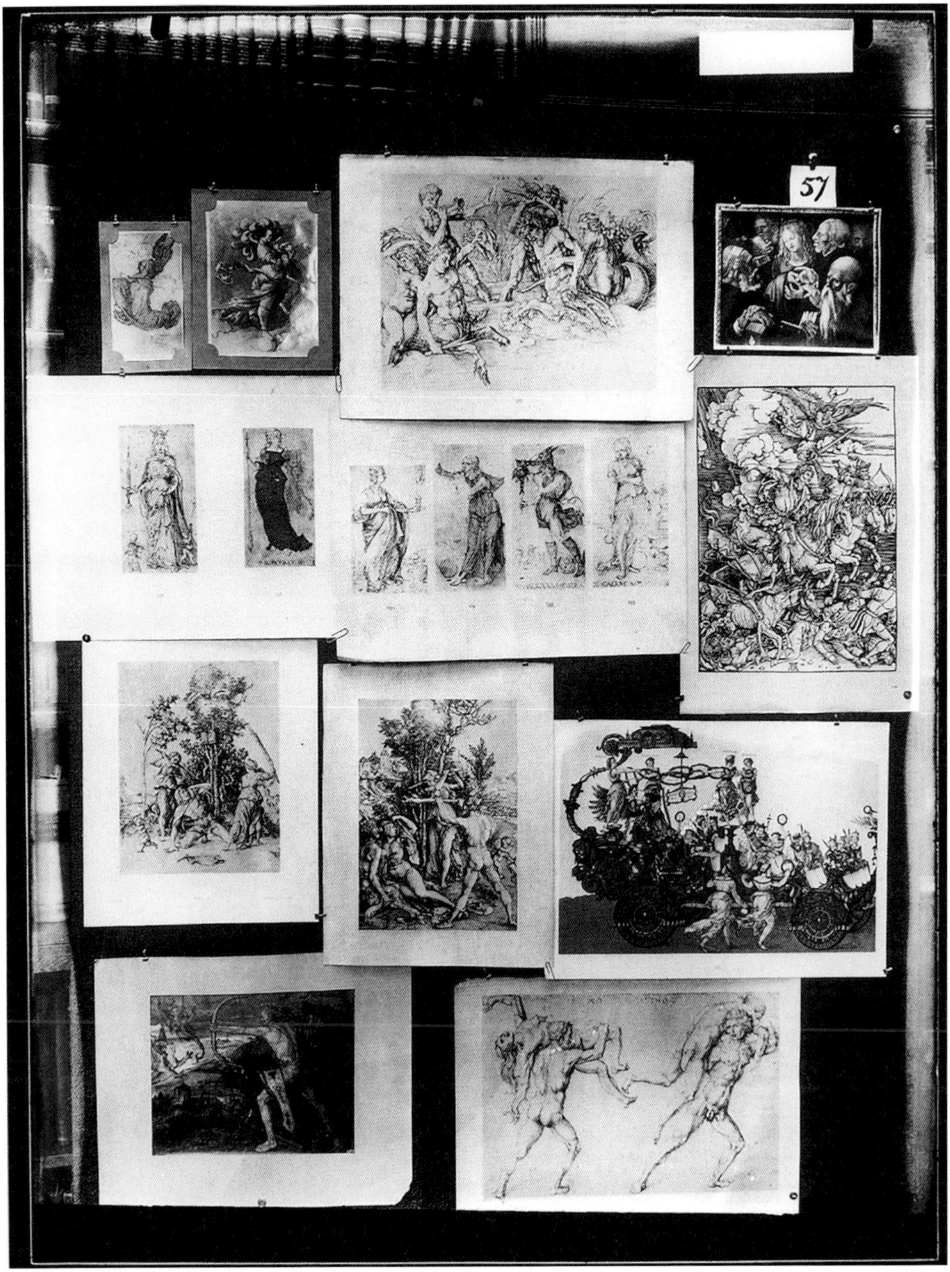

Aby Warburg, *Mnemosyne Atlas*, Panel 5

facsimiles of Warburg's panels, but rather represent the same artworks using different images gleaned from a variety of historical sources — which is significant in that it maintains Warburg's focus on the multiplicities of representation, and how an individual work of art will, over time, be subject to continuous change: it is never a stable object, but rather an unstable one, images multiplying and circulating as the infrastructure and platforms for their dissemination expand and change with time. And it is the instability of the representation that is a cornerstone tenet of all cultural transmission.[3]

One distinguishing mark of Warburg's process is the vague sources of the images that comprise each panel: they are images without origins. We can usually identify what is being represented by the images; but the books these images are from, the newspapers, and other sources, are often less clear. As images are dispersed in culture, and images derive from images, the sense of filiation becomes important as a way of establishing the relative authority between each image. In literary studies, one of the oldest subdisciplines is known as textual criticism: it goes back as far as the Library of Alexandria, when attempts were made to map the trajectory of Homer's texts. To do this textual criticism developed a practice known as 'recension', or 'stemmatics', with maps of textual genealogies showing how one text derived from another. Surprisingly, the discipline has not translated well to art history, where relatively scant attention has been paid to the genealogy of images that derive from, or are based upon, individual works of art. Art history generally takes these images for granted, even where the images migrate and morph in terms of color and scale. The 21st century has evolved as the age of the authorless image. Digital cutting and pasting has created a culture of iterable representations, and our global critical discourse is built up around these images. 'Originals' rarely matter when art is being read as a social experience, and even in much academic discourse today, critical commentary is based on representations.

For both Warburg and Shams, their respective projects can be described as studies in the rhetoric of visual presentation. They are projects that study images as images, and how they might be organized outside of the structures of a logocentric mode of reading. In his seminal book *Interaction of Color*, which was published in 1963, Josef Albers wrote that you cannot put one color beside another without also changing both. By extension, you cannot put one image beside another without also changing both — and in *Peter the Great*, Shams draws out, teases out, this sense in which every image generates a comment on the images beside it. The process is one that involves activating images as dynamic relationships. These positionings and juxtapositionings often seem arbitrary, but they are not. Instead, the images are continually repositioned in relation to different schemas for the organization of the collection, and the same documents get reorganized into different arrangements and different narratives, finally imploding into a tangle of human subjectivity. It's not so much the totality of the system that matters, but the way a comparative analysis — like Michel Adanson's — makes meaning out of relationships. Ezra Pound has a relevant comment about this in his *ABC of Reading*, which, while ostensibly about reading literature, is also important to the process of reading images: "The proper METHOD for studying poetry and good letters is the method of contemporary biologists, that is careful first-hand examination of the matter, and continual COMPARISON of one 'slide' or specimen with another."[4]

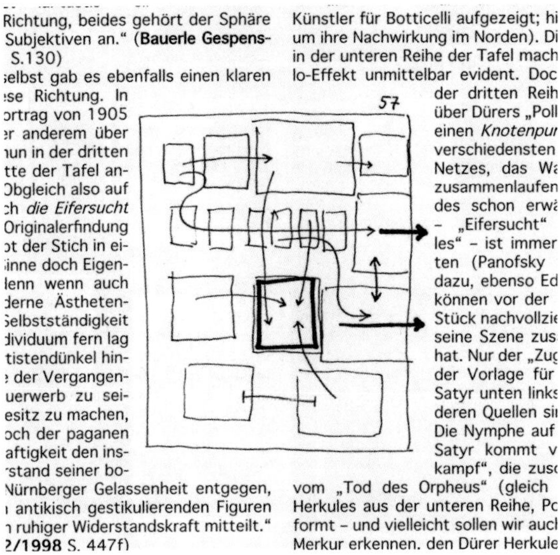

Richtung, beides gehört der Sphäre
Subjektiven an.“ (**Bauerle Gespens-**
S.130)
selbst gab es ebenfalls einen klaren
se Richtung. In
ortrag von 1905
er anderem über
un in der dritten
tte der Tafel an-
Obgleich also auf
ch *die Eifersucht*
Originalerfindung
ot der Stich in ei-
inne doch Eigen-
lenn wenn auch
derne Ästheten-
Selbstständigkeit
dividuum fern lag
tistendünkel hin-
der Vergangen-
uerwerb zu sei-
esitz zu machen,
och der paganen
aftigkeit den ins-
stand seiner bo-
Nürnberger Gelassenheit entgegen,
antikisch gestikulierenden Figuren
n ruhiger Widerstandskraft mitteilt.“
2/1998 S. 447f)

Künstler für Botticelli aufgezeigt; hi
um ihre Nachwirkung im Norden). Di
in der unteren Reihe der Tafel mach
lo-Effekt unmittelbar evident. Doc
der dritten Reih
über Dürers „Poll
einen *Knotenpu*
verschiedensten
Netzes, das Wa
zusammenlaufen
des schon erwä
– „Eifersucht“
les“ – ist immer
ten (Panofsky
dazu, ebenso Ed
können vor der
Stück nachvollzie
seine Szene zus
hat. Nur der „Zug
der Vorlage für
Satyr unten links
deren Quellen si
Die Nymphe auf
Satyr kommt v
kampf“, die zus
vom „Tod des Orpheus“ (gleich
Herkules aus der unteren Reihe, Pc
formt – und vielleicht sollen wir auc
Merkur erkennen, den Dürer Herkule

Mnemosyne: Der Bilderatlas von Aby Warburg.
Eine Rekonstruktion im 8. Salon, Teil 8. Nr. 10.2.
Ed. Roberto Ohrt and Phillipp Schwalb
(St. Gallen: Kulturraum St. Gallen, 2016), np

Warburg's *Mnemosyne* panels were developed between 1924-1929; Pound's *ABC of Reading* was first published in 1934. Both so close in time, and both so close in their emphasis on comparative analysis. A line of Keats beside a line of Shelley beside a line of Wallace Stevens is an arrangement of intertextual relations. Similarly, Warburg's *Atlas* and Shams' *Peter The Great* can be described as exhibitions of intertextual grids: projected on the wall, laid flat on tables, bound up into books. The grid is perhaps our most efficient and practical infrastructure for visual rhetoric. Historically, the grid sought to escape from content: for Agnes Martin and Sol Lewitt, the grid was formalized, emptied of everything except itself. But with Albers, the grid became subject to a different kind of scrutiny, the relationship between one color and another. It was later in the 20th century that the grid of photographic images evolved as a narrative device. Gerhard Richter's *Atlas* project is most often cited as an evolutionary turn from Warburg[5], but the work of Douglas Blau, as one example, and Henrik Olesen, as another, offer more evolved instances of the potential of the grid.[6] In the hands of artists, Warburg's methodology becomes a form of institutional critique by using art history against itself. Rarely is this position a vocalized claim by the artists, yet it is one of those implied gestures that demonstrates how easily art transcends the intentions of its makers. Both Warburg and Shams show us how our collective social memory is a memory of conflicting assemblages, where events, objects, and images of them are reshaped and reorganized into collective re-remembering. The homogeneous society gives way to the heterogeneous individual. The monumental gives way to its pictorial representation. In the end what is left is not an assigned order of images, but the seemingly random displacement that revels in the moment, then diffuses into another state of being. ●

1 – *The Diary of John Evelyn*, ed. E.S. de Beer (London: Oxford University Press, 1959), p. 301.

2 – Douglas Blau, *Alexis Rockman* (New York and Los Angeles: Jay Gorney Modern Art and Thomas Solomon's Garage, 1992): np.

3 – I discuss this more expansively in *Textualterity: Art, Theory, And Textual Criticism* (Ann Arbor, Mi.: University of Michigan Press, 1995).

4 – Ezra Pound, *ABC of Reading.* (1934; Rpt. New Directions, 1960), p.17.

5 – Benjamin H.D. Buchloh, 'Gerhard Richter's "Atlas": The Anomic Archive', *October 88* (1999), p.117-145.

6 – Douglas Blau, *Douglas Blau / curated by Ingrid Schaffner* (Philadelphia: Institute of Contemporary Art, 2008); Henrik Olesen, *Some Faggy Gestures*, Heike Munder (ed), (Zürich: JRP | Ringier, 2008).

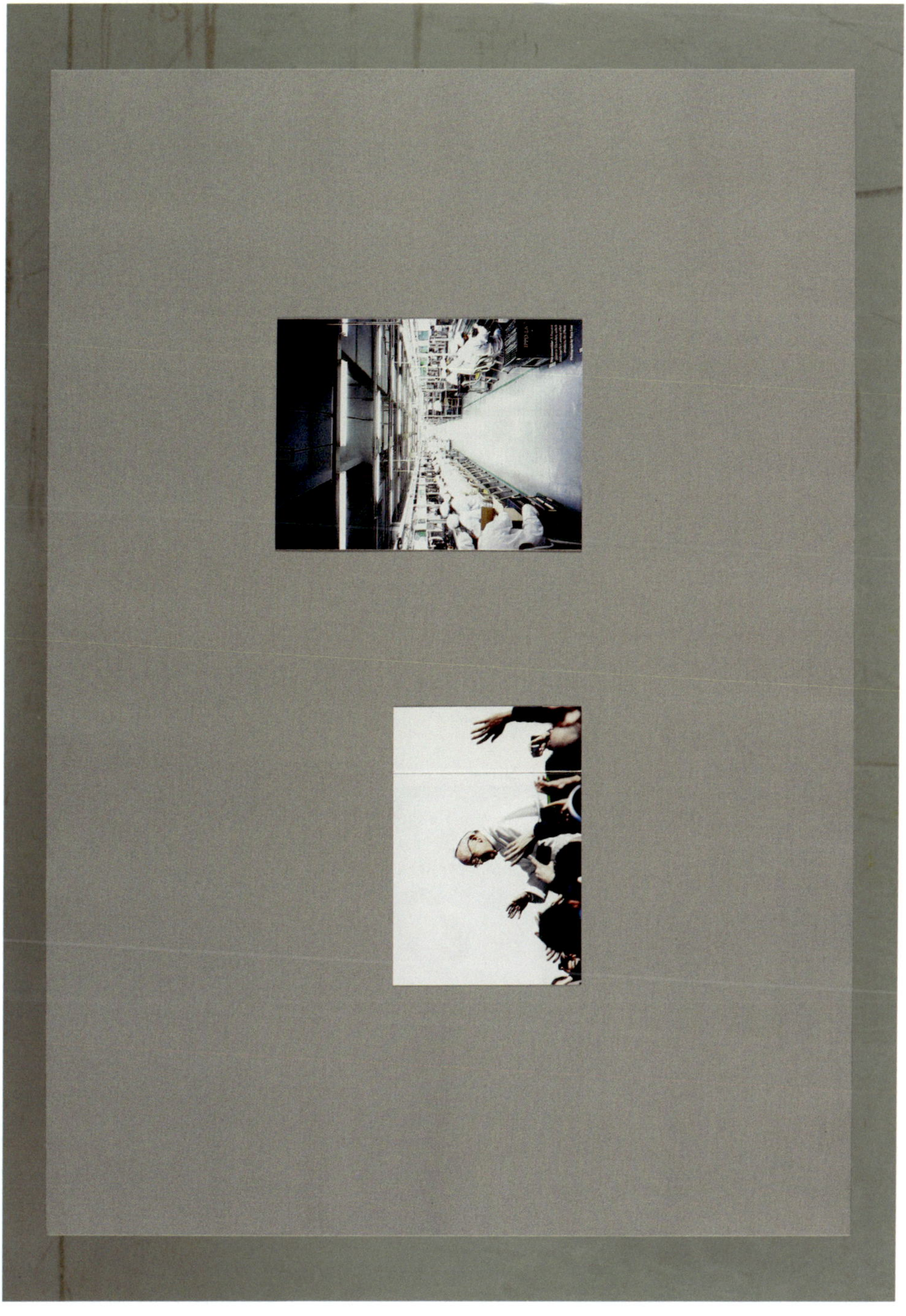

back (plate 2) [MA]

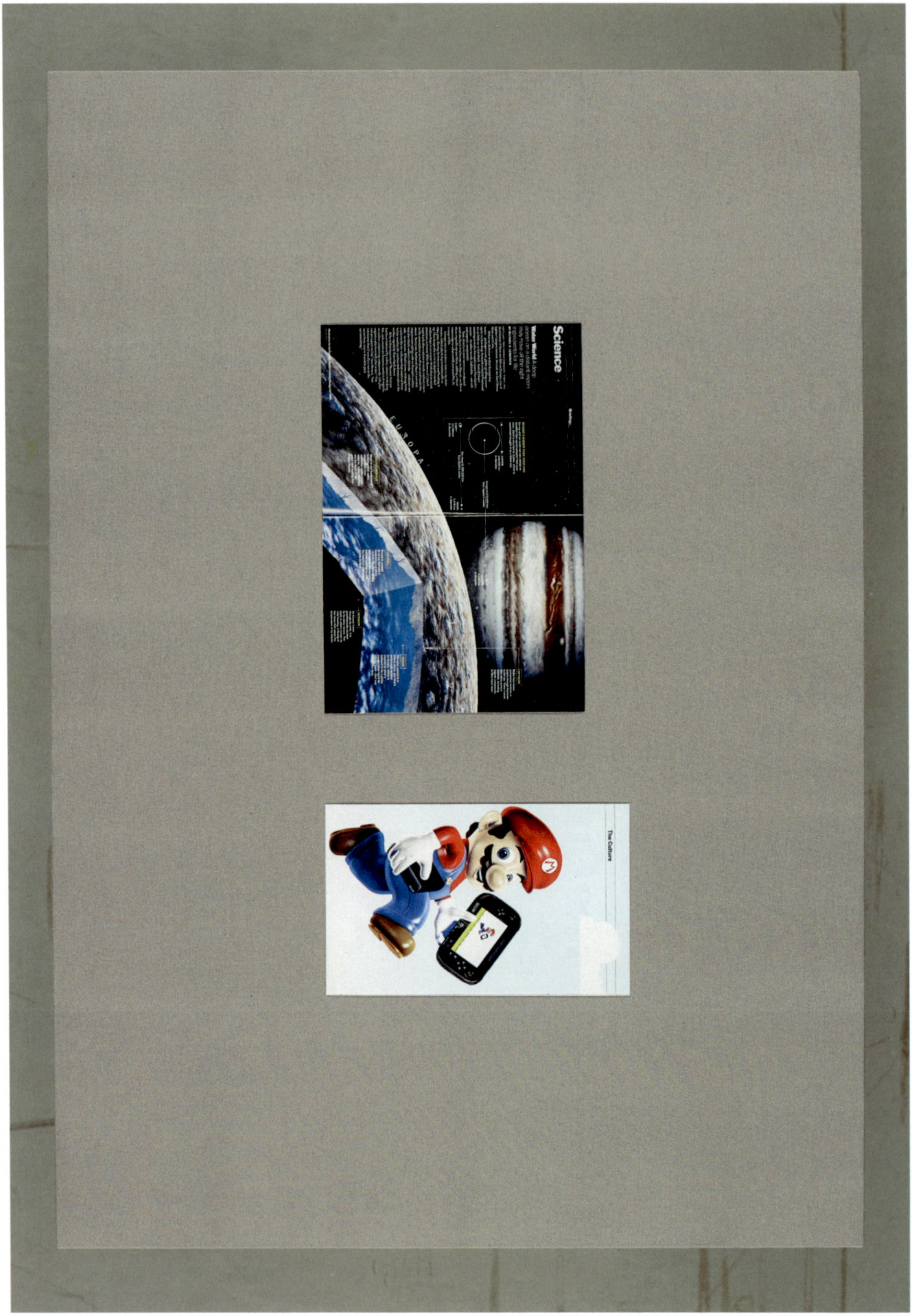
Science
EUROPA
The Culture

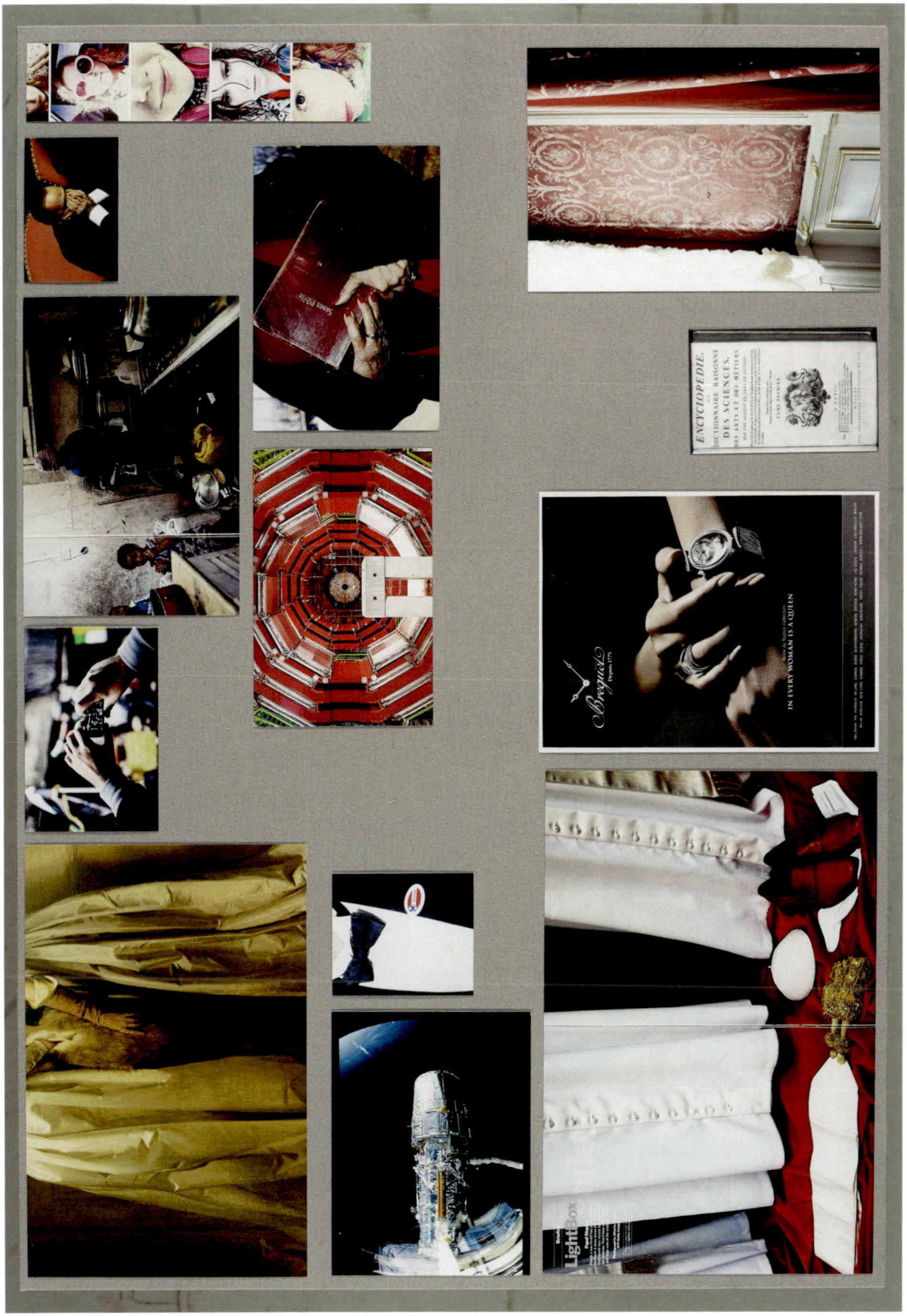

cropped image [MA]

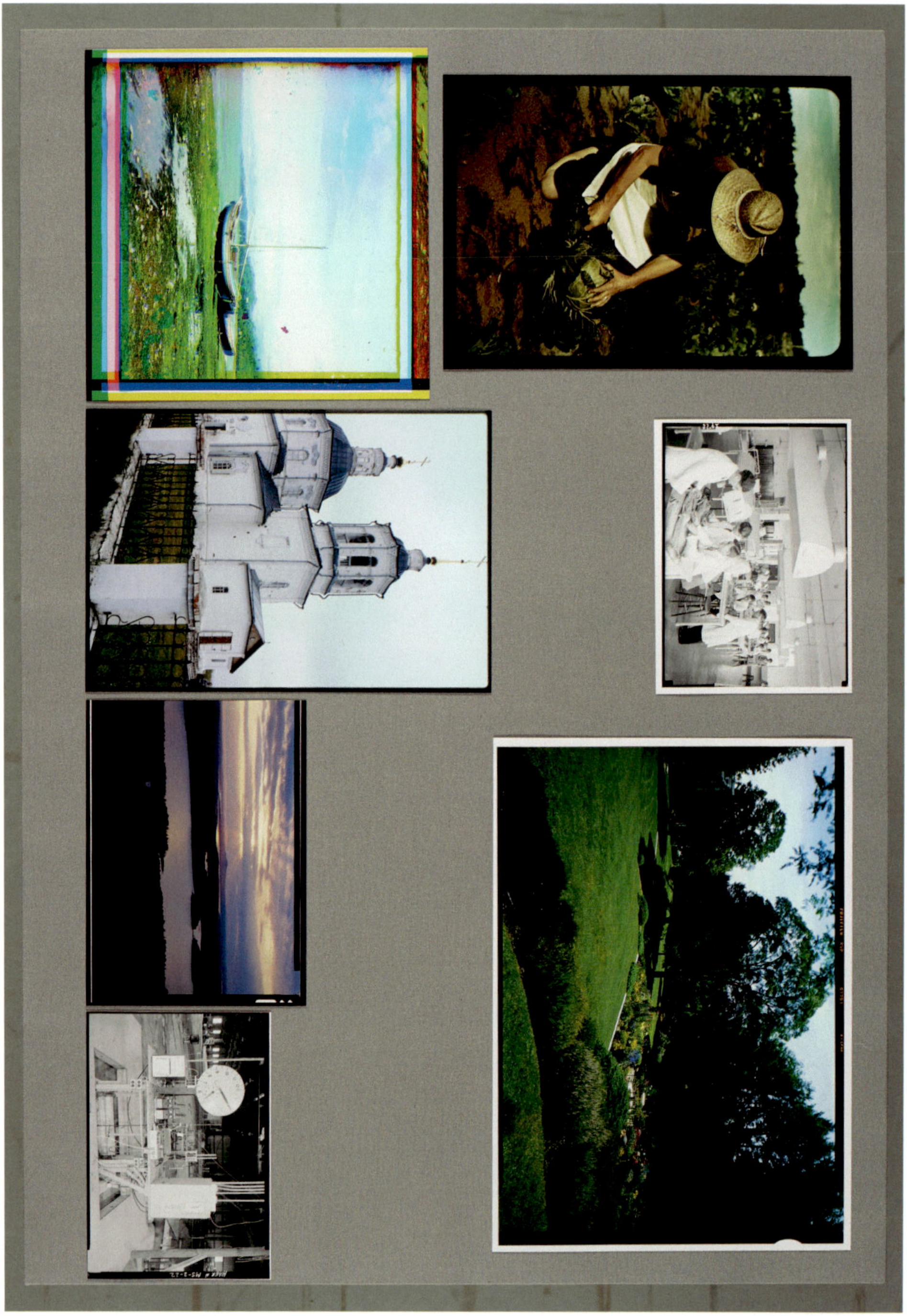

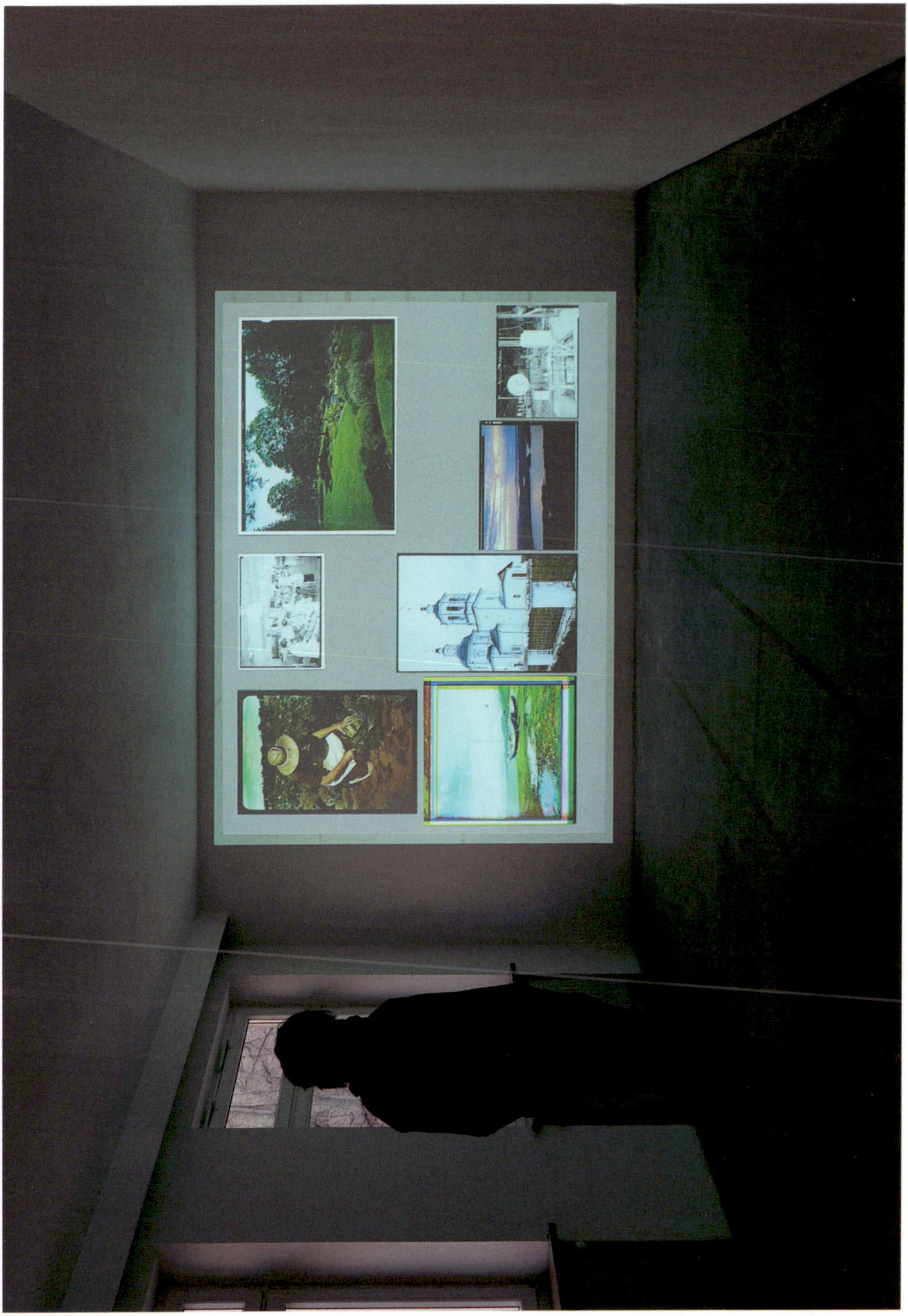

Installation view, Kunstraum München 2016

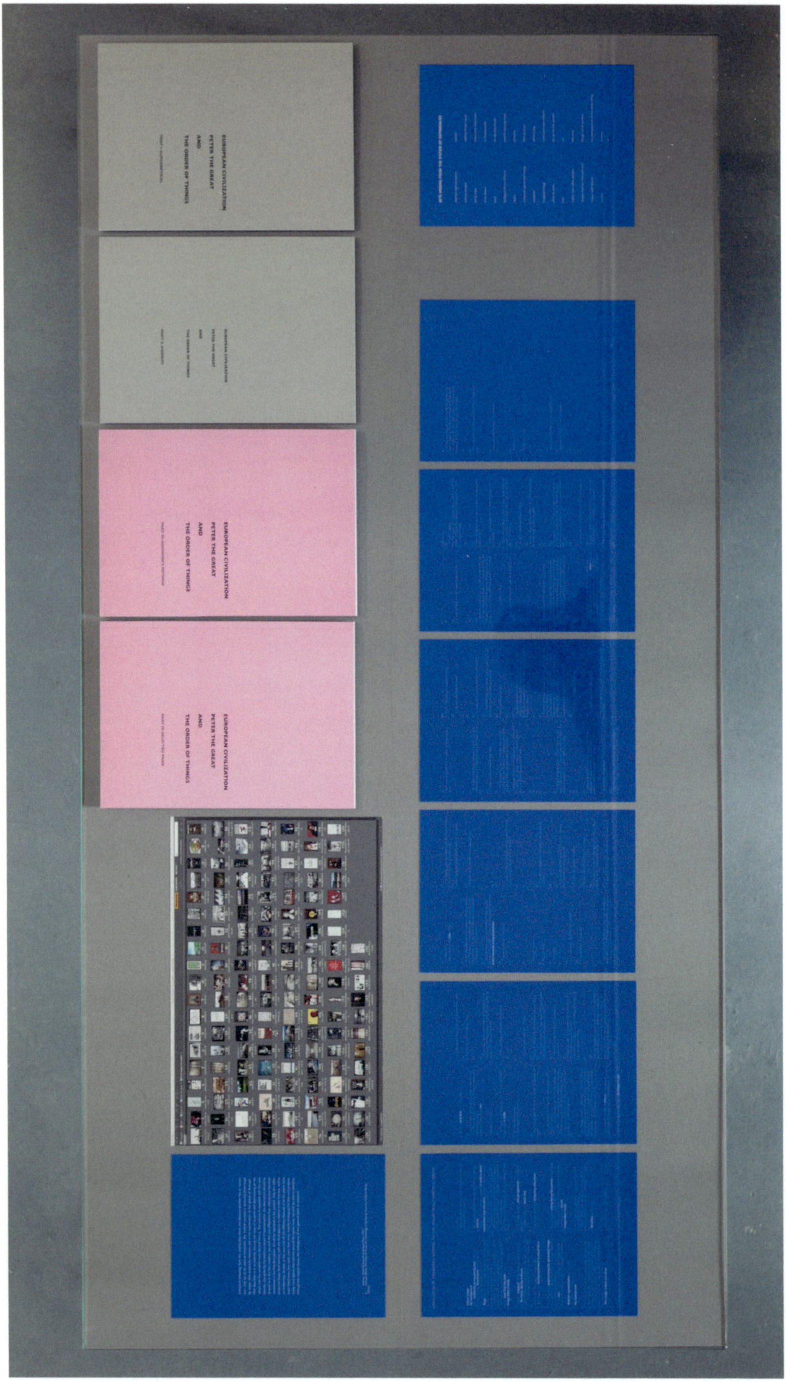

Installation view, Kunstakademie Düsseldorf

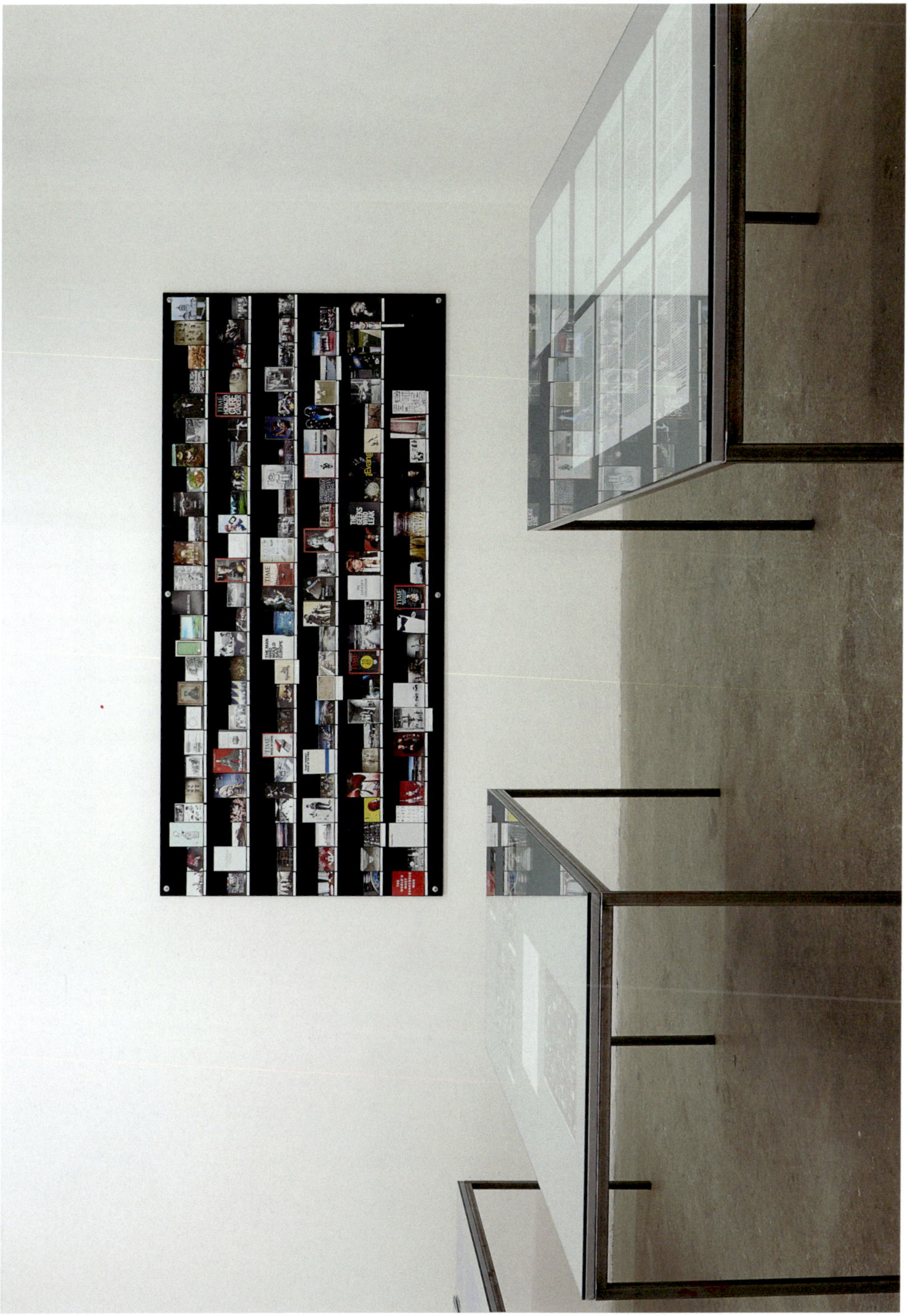

Installation view, Kunstraum München 2016

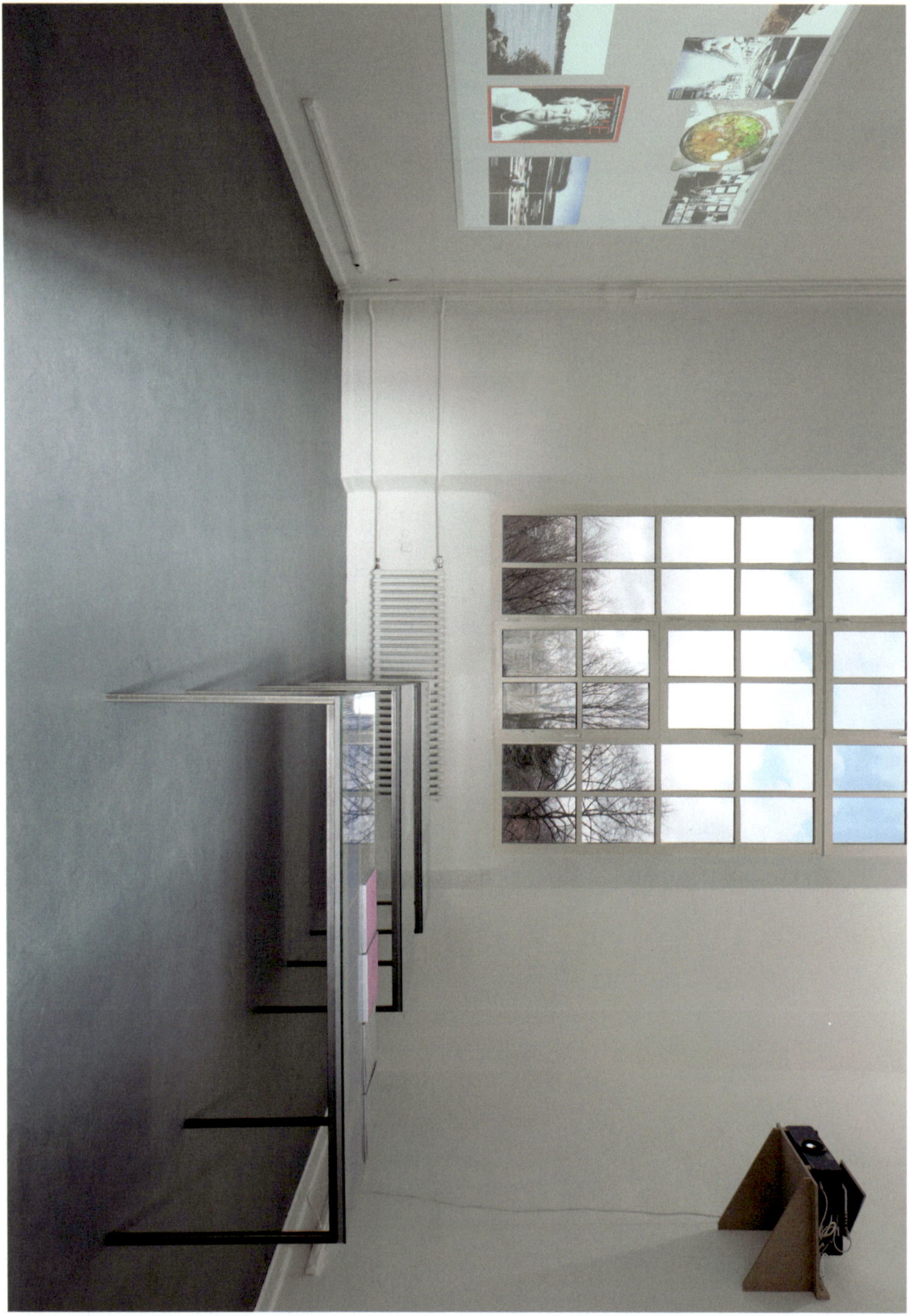

Installation view, Kunstakademie Düsseldorf

„[...] if photography is a mapping of bodies in time and space, then it is also a production of both those bodies and modernity's particular conception of the time-space continuum."
– Geoffrey Batchen[1]

Christina Irrgang

VISUELLER TOTALITÄT BEGEGNEN

Über die künstlerische Arbeit von Fari Shams

Wir kommunizieren durch Sprache und durch Bilder. Doch weder Sprache, noch Bilder folgen demselben System, auch dann nicht, wenn sie sich innerhalb eines Kulturkreises bewegen. Die Vieldeutigkeit des (Bild-)Sprachlichen impliziert gleichermaßen die Vielschichtigkeit von Systemen, durch welche Sprache und Bilder in ihrem jeweiligen Kontext erschlossen werden, ja, durch welche sie *eine* Ordnung erfahren. Ordnung ist niemals absolut, denn auch sie ist an eine Systematik gebunden, die von Situation zu Situation variiert. Ein Ordnungssystem führt nur dann zu einer Synthese, wenn es in seinem jeweiligen Kontext strukturbildend ist, das heißt, wenn es die Logik der Situation trägt und verstärkt. Ordnung ist in ihrer Essenz niemals hierarchisch: sondern spezifisch abstrakt, reflexiv. Das System jedoch, das sie klassifiziert, bildet eine Hierarchie, nimmt der Ordnung ihre Demokratie. Klassifizierung wird bestimmt durch einen Entscheidungsträger, demnach ist ihr Charakter subjektiv. Doch auch die subjektive Entscheidung folgt einer vorgegebenen Struktur. Ordnungssysteme sind immer wahr, und zugleich nie.

Sprache und Bilder, literarische und wissenschaftliche Texte, Schrift und Zeitschriften, Bildarchive und Räume, die einer Ordnung folgen, das sind Parameter, mit denen Fari Shams arbeitet. Die Betrachtung von Bild-Text-Verhältnissen, ja die narrative (An-)Ordnung und Ausrichtung von Bild und Sprache formen dabei eine wiederkehrende Thematik in ihrer künstlerischen Arbeit. So heißt die Installation, über die und in der wir uns 2012 kennen lernten: *The Order of Things*. Die Arbeit besteht aus einer Soundinstallation und einem Künstlerbuch. Durch Sprache, Grafik, Reproduktion und fotografisches Reenactment wird Alain Robbe Grillets Text *THREE REFLECTED VISIONS - The Dressmaker's Dummy* auf einer Metaebene konzeptuell und medienanalytisch reflektiert. Im Ausstellungsraum[2] wurde ich von einer aufgenommenen Stimme umgeben, die Narration zirkulierte szenisch um mich herum: Beschreibungen eines abwesenden Raumes innerhalb des realen Raumes, Koordinaten durch Worte bildend. Im Künstlerbuch dann den Raum durch aufklappbare Seiten fortbildend und spiegelnd, mittels fotografischer Situationen und analytischer Textexzerpte das Spektrum erweiternd, prismatisch weitend.

Fari Shams fächert Ordnungssysteme auf und sie erzeugt *Gegenbilder* durch das Duplizieren des Bildhaften. Ihren Arbeiten wohnt dabei eine „apparative Autonomie“[3] inne: Fotografie ist in ihrem Werk formbildend, doch synthetisiert die Künstlerin das Fotografische in Hinblick auf dessen bildproduzierende Komponenten. Shams agiert, mit Vilém Flusser gesporchen, „für eine Philosophie der Fotografie“, im Bewusstsein die Frage nach der Freiheit in einem Kontext[4], der durch das fotografische Agieren erst entsteht. Wenn die Existenz zwischen Chaos und apparatischer Systembildung pendelt, wie können wir noch Freiheit in ihr finden und uns selbst verorten, respektive einen (Lebens-)Raum geben? „Freiheit ist, gegen den Apparat zu spielen.“[5]

Das Medium Buch dient der Künstlerin oft als Reflexions- und Präsentationmedium, so auch in ihrer Arbeit *European Civilization, Peter the Great, and The Order of Things* (2014), die Ausgangspunkt und Gegenstand der folgenden Überlegungen ist. Den Corpus der Arbeit bilden vier Bücher, die nach verschiedenen Ordnungssystemen eine feststehende Menge fotografischer Abbildungen strukturieren. Die Quellen der fotografischen Reproduktionen sind analog und digital, sie sind Metaphern für das Alltägliche und das Überlieferte. Zum einen besteht dieses Material aus Auszügen aus dem US-amerikanischen Magazin *TIME* aus dem Jahrgang 2012. Diese Exzerpte – einzelne Fotografien, ganzseitige Artikel, Werbeanzeigen, Typografie, Grafiken oder Cover des Magazins – erweitert Shams durch eine Auswahl aus der Bilddatenbank des Internet-Archivs der Library of Congress, der weltweit größten Bibliothek mit Sitz in Washington, D.C. Insgesamt sind es 145 Bilder, die Fari Shams zunächst auf der digitalen Fläche zusammen führt, und nach verschiedenen Methoden und in unterschiedlichen Medien rekontextualisiert. Da ist das Noticeboard, welches die 145 Abbildungen wie die Buchstaben eines Alphabets dokumentiert. Befinden wir uns im Ausstellungsraum, werden diese Abbildungen in verschiedenen Systematiken dargelegt und dem Noticeboard als rückbezügliche Quelle gegenüber gestellt. Eine Projektion zeigt in 40 Ansichten unterschiedliche Bildkombinationen. Eine Folge an Tischen wiederum trägt Texte, Bildpanels und die zuvor erwähnten Bücher. Um diese vierteilige Buchfolge soll es im Folgenden gehen, denn sie legt anhand von vier angewandten Methoden Fari Shams‘ reflexives Bildsystem dar.

So zeigt das erste Buch eine alphabetische Ordnung der Bilder, die sich an ihren jeweiligen Bildunterschriften orientiert. Im zweiten Band sind Shams‘ Bildexzerpte nach Denis Diderots *Map of the System of Human Knowledge* (1750) sortiert, während der dritte Band einer ethnografisch-botanischen Kategorisierung nach Michel Adanson (*Familles naturelles des plantes*, 1763, siehe Seite 74) folgt. Der vierte Band wiederum vereint ausgewählte Paare in der Gegenüberstellung. Die Gesamtauswahl der 145 Bilder führt zurück auf die Kristallisation von Schlagworten, hervorgehend aus einem Vortrag von John Merriman über Peter den Großen, von dem sich auch der Titel der Arbeit ableitet: *European Civilization 1648-1945*. Die Vorlesung des Historikers Merriman, die er an der Yale-University abgehalten hat, war Teil einer Reihe, doch bildet sie in Fari Shams‘ Arbeit eine Art Colophon, das durch das Hervorheben der verschiedenen Schlagworte zu einem vorgelagerten Narrativ sowie Index der Arbeit *European Civilization, Peter the Great, and The Order of Things* wird.

Das Reformdenken des Peter des Großen, der sich an westlichen Codes zur Erzeugung eines modernen, aufgeklärten russischen Staates orientierte, ist in *European Civilization, Peter the*

Great, and The Order of Things in einer Linie mit dem sinnbildlichen, fotografischen Vermitteln von westlichen Werten durch westlich geprägte Bildkanäle zu sehen. Während Peter der Große (1672-1725) in einer Zeit lebte, in der Bilder im Plural gerade als neue Form der Betrachtung en vogue waren, wie zum Beispiel in den niederländischen Galeriedarstellungen des David Teniers', bewegen wir uns heute in einem Kosmos, der nahezu ausschließlich auf einer bilddialogischen Kommunikation basiert. Fotografien sind dabei Schnittstellen zwischen Kapitalismus und Kontrolle. Sie steuern Bewusstsein und kapitalistisches Verhalten, oder, mit Geoffrey Batchen gesprochen, „[...] the meaning of every photograph is imbricated within broader social and political forces."[6] Wie fließen umgekehrt diese als Bildsysteme vermittelten Werte wieder in die kapitalistische Gesellschaft ein? Shams richtet den Blick auf die zeitgenössischen sozialen, politischen und kulturellen Implikationen mit ihrem fotografischen Querschnitt aus einem Jahr *TIME Magazine*, und hinterfragt zugleich in Hinblick auf selektive archivarische Prozesse die durch das digitale Bildarchiv transportierten und verkörperten Werte. „What is the photograph on the inside, before it enters a specific historical and political context?"[7] Diese von Geoffrey Batchen formulierte Frage steht auch hier im Raum.

Fari Shams arbeitet mit ihrer kritischen Bildinvestigation ihrerseits aufklärend, und schaltet ihrem Bilddiskurs Michel Foucaults philosophisch-theoretischen Ansatz seines Buches *Die Ordnung der Dinge* quer. Foucaults Verhandlung von Worten und Dingen bildet dabei die Grundlage eines vernetzten Denkens, wie es sich in Shams' Arbeit in Form von Systemen zur Erzeugung von Bild-Enzyklopädien sowie einer bildbasierten Analyse gesellschaftlicher sowie kulturell determinierter Systeme ausdrückt.

Shams' vierteilige Buchfolge *European Civilization, Peter the Great, and The Order of Things* nimmt die Funktion eines heterotopen Ortes ein.[8] Es ist ein Ort der fixierten Betrachtung von fluktuierenden Bildern, die durch vier verschiedene Systematiken, ja Mechanismen, je spezifische Bildzusammenschlüsse als Bildtafeln bilden. Dabei arbeitet die Künstlerin bildarchäologisch, und untersucht in der Remontage global distribuierter fotografischer Ansichten ihre kulturellen Codes. Fari Shams bezieht sich zunächst auf Diderots *Map of the System of Human Knowledge*, wodurch sich menschliches Begreifen durch Erinnerung, Ratio und Vorstellung, durch Geschichte, Philosophie und Poesie zusammenfügt. So bilden *memory*, *reason* und *imagination* Kategorien für Shams' Bildkartei, reflektierend über Zivilisation, menschliche Kommunikationsstrukturen und die Herausbildung von (fotografischen) Narrativen. Die Fotografien erscheinen in *European Civilization, Peter the Great, and The Order of Things* dabei immer wieder als Modelle – für Erleben, Erkennen, Werten und Handeln.[9] Die Künstlerin hinterfragt diese Archetypenbildung, indem sie selbst daran anknüpfende Kategorisierungen schafft: sie organisieren, was sich innerhalb ihrer Ordnung befindet, und schließen aus, was darin nicht zu integrieren ist.[10] Die Fotografie wird dabei zu einem Medium des Speicher(n)s, des Inventarisierens, der Ordnung und der Systematisierung[11]: eine Enzyklopädie, welche einerseits Sichtmomente vorgibt, doch welche durch Fari Shams' spezifische Systemzuordnungen je nach Kontext anderen Parametern folgt. Shams' zitierte Systeme bilden in ihrer Summe ein System der Hinterfragung.

Die Wiederkehr des Bildes und dessen Neuplatzierung dienen Fari Shams so als Struktur und Methode. Eine Besonderheit bildet hierbei Buch III unter Rückgriff auf Adansons *Familles naturelles des plantes*, ein Notationssystem über Pflanzen im Senegal, das er 1763 verfasste. So wendet Shams Adansons Methode auf die 145 Bilder an, indem sie jene – der alphabetischen Zuordnung des ersten Buches folgend – der Reihe nach beschreibt, ohne dabei Beschreibungen in ihrer Spezifik zu wiederholen. Die so entstehenden Differenzen bilden in ihrer Benennung Charakteristiken heraus, die als Grundlage der weiteren Bildkategorisierung dienen. Damit schaffen die neu gebildeten Termini also auch die Kategorien für die Formation der in Band III zusammen geführten Bildgruppen. Die Bilder folgen einem System, das auf Sprache basiert, doch entgrenzen sie in ihrer Präsentation jegliche Verbalisierung. Sprache und Bild sind hier in einer Art „double bind" miteinander verbunden: sie bedingen einander und schließen sich zugleich in ihrer Repräsentation gegenseitig aus. Dabei entsteht eine dem Visuellen inhärente duale Ideologie: ein visueller Antagonismus, bei dem Bild gegen Bild[12] agiert. Eine Tableau-Sprache nach Foucault, „jetzt ist die Sprache Bild."[13] Wohingegen das technische, also fotografische Bild nach Vilém Flusser, immer nur auf Sprache bzw. sprachlich überlieferten Systemen basiert, einem nachalphabetischen Code folgend. Adansons Methode erscheint schließlich in Fari Shams' Anwendung nicht nur tautologisch, sondern als „mise en abyme" – ein Bild im Bild, das sich stets selbst enthält.

Mit *European Civilization, Peter the Great, and The Order of Things* generiert Fari Shams einen Bildatlas, der zweifelsohne als konzeptioneller und ästhetischer Anklang an Aby Warburgs *Mnemosyne* und dessen mit Stoff bespannte analytische Bildtafeln zu sehen ist, an welche beispielsweise auch die Textur des Bildhintergrundes bei Shams' Bildarrangements erinnert. Doch zugleich ist Shams' Arbeit ein bild-politischer Reader, dessen Bilddaten ein arbiträres Surrogat aus online akkumulierter Archivdaten und einer Vielzahl an Ausgaben der (Nachrichten-)Zeitschrift *TIME* verkörpern, aus der weltweit Bevölkerungskreise subjektiv ihre Weltbilder beziehen, nachdem diese nach spezifischen Methoden und Systemen aufbereitet wurden. Susan Sontag schreibt: „Es ist immer ein Bild, das jemand gewählt hat; Fotografieren heißt einen Ausschnitt wählen, und einen Ausschnitt wählen heißt ausschließen."[14] Judith Butler führt diesen Gedanken noch weiter: „Es bedarf keiner Bildunterschrift und keines Narrativs, um zu begreifen, dass der Rahmen [die Wahl des fotografischen Ausschnitts, Anm. d. A.] explizit einen politischen Hintergrund formuliert und verlängert"[15] – im Kontext der Fotografie, wie auch im Bereich der Bildredaktion oder der Konstruktion eines Archivs. Fari Shams greift diesen Prozess auf, trifft editorische Entscheidungen und erzeugt eine dialektische Spannung, indem sie fragmentiert und neu platziert – nicht zuletzt im vierten Band der Buchfolge, anhand ausgewählter Bildpaare. Dabei treten einzelne Bilder in eine komparative Beziehung, wobei Shams diese Bilder wiederholt und in jeweils neuen Konstellationen dialogisch zusammensetzt: Sie bilden eine Dialektik, bei der „jedes Element als eigenständiges Subjekt der Rede"[16] erscheint, sie aber im Gesamten ein Narrativ erzeugen, das auf dem Seriellen basiert. „Wenn Dinge wiederholt werden", kommentiert Hans-Peter Feldmann in Bezug zu fotografischen Bildern, „entsteht ein Durchschnittswert, der richtiger ist, als es ein einzelnes Bild je sein kann."[17] Oder so: Die Wiederholung der Bilder multipliziert die Möglichkeit ihrer Ansicht.

Die von der Künstlerin ausgewählten Bild-Exzerpte formulieren dabei einen auf Subjektivität basierenden Daten-Pool, der als Mikrosystem streng genommen auch dem Datenraum des Internets gleicht, in dem die technische Funktion – gekoppelt an eine subjektive Suche –

Bilder punktuell hervor holt und systembedingt rekombiniert. Doch die endlose Verfügbarkeit wird hier durch eine klar formulierte Auswahl gebrochen. Shams' vierteilige Buchfolge formatiert dabei „das Oszillieren der Bilder zwischen digitalem Raum und Buchraum“[18], während die Künstlerin die Grenzen zwischen analogem und digitalem Archiv sowohl innerhalb ihrer Bücher, als auch im Format der Ausstellung zwischen Publikation und Projektion nivelliert. „Photography will [...] lose its power as a privileged conveyor of information. Given the proliferation of digital images that look exactly like photographs, photography may even be robbed of its cultural identity as a distinctive medium“, schreibt Geoffrey Batchen.[19] Und so reflektiert Fari Shams metamedial die visuelle Matrix eines globalen Archivs, indem sie ihm selbst Systematiken verordnet und „kontrollierte“ Wahrnehmung zwischen Orientierung und Chaos – als *temporäre* Matrix[20] – auffächert.

Sie bildet Konstellationen und Allianzen, kehrt die kontextuelle Verortung von Bildern hervor und erzeugt selbst Kontexte, die u.a. Kirche und Militär, Weltordnungen und Handlungsräume, Technologie und Marketing, Gender und Klischees thematisieren. Die Künstlerin arbeitet dabei auch mit den Faktoren Zeit und Erinnerung, ganz ähnlich, wie sie durch Diderot in *Map of the System of Human Knowledge* beschrieben werden. Welche Bilder prägen sich ein und welche vermittelten Gesten geraten in Vergessenheit? Das Materielle und das Kulturelle verschränken sich: „Photography as something that is simultaneously material and cultural, manifested as much in the attributes of the photographic object as in its contextualisation. Philosophy has a word for all this: deconstruction.“[21]

Die Dekonstruktion wird so schließlich in der Auswahl von nur 40 Bildtafeln aus 212 Bildkombinationen bei der Projektion im Ausstellungsraum am deutlichsten. Während sich Fari Shams' vierteilige Buchfolge in ihrer Bildenzyklopädie immer wieder auf einen vollständigen Bildwert – nämlich dem inhärenten Ausgangswert 145 – beziehen, besteht die Projektion in ihrer Selektion als Auflösung dieses Bildkörpers. Die Projektion wird zur Metapher für die Unvollständigkeit, für den Verlust von Daten und Informationen. Sie zeigt das Poröse eines jeden Systems, die Fragilität der Repräsentation. Sie wird zur Paraphrase der Buchfolge.

Das Archiv, dessen Neuordnung sowie Unvollständigkeit ist eine Thematik, die Fari Shams wiederkehrend in ihrer künstlerischen Arbeit verhandelt. So bildet das Projekt respektive das Buch *The Concise Companion to Art History arranged by Ingo Müller and Gerd Schneider* (2014) ein Archiv aus Bilddateien ab, die Shams im mittlerweile unbenutzten Dia-Archiv der Düsseldorfer Kunstakademie gefunden, und anschließend mittels Suchmaschine im Internet digital rekonstruiert hat. Dabei wird insbesondere die Leerstelle sowie die Auflösung einer alphabetischen oder thematischen Ordnung strukturbildend, war diese im physischen, lückenhaften Lichtbild-Archiv nicht mehr ersichtlich. Die Dekonstruktion wie auch die Rekonstruktion des Archivs wurde damit zum Ausgangspunkt für Fari Shams' Publikation. Hier zeigt sich: In De- und Rekonstruktion wird der Begriff des Archives brüchig, wenn es nur mehr Exzerpt ist. „That which survives in the archives does so by chance. Disappearance is the rule“, kommentiert Susan Buck-Morss zum ephemeren Archiv, und skizziert den Zufall als regelnde Komponente.[22] So wird in Shams' Arbeit deutlich, dass Kategorie und Methodik zur analytischen Beurteilung von Bildern unumgänglich ist, aber dass Kategorie und Methodik Variablen – wie die des Verschwindens – bilden können, die im virtuellen Raum des

Internets ihre zeitgenössische Entsprechung finden: mit der subjektiven Enzyklopädie als Resultat. Fari Shams reflektiert in ihrer Arbeit so immer wieder auch die Lückenhaftigkeit, die eine im Volumen gestiegene, aber durch kategoriale Selektion determinierte, zeitgenössische Bildwahrnehmung kennzeichnet.

Hier, bei *European Civilization, Peter the Great, and The Order of Things*, wird der Körper des Archivs zu einer Kartei von Bildern zwischen Populismus und Historizität[23], die dem Prozess einer prä-narrativen Zensur entstammen und mit der Buchfolge und der Projektion als post-narrative Sequenz verwendet werden. Sie bilden ein fotografisches Dispositiv. Shams' Bildgruppen spiegeln dabei zelluloidhaft eine visuelle Totalität, die sich seit der technischen Reproduzierbarkeit von Bildern über verschiedene Publikationskanäle, Bildträger und technische Potentiale auffächert, von fotografischen Reproduktionen über das Bewegtbild und fotobasierte Medien bis hin zum digitalen Bild im Internet. Technisch produzierte Bilder, nach Vilém Flusser sogenannte Technobilder, zirkulierten zu keiner Zeit stärker, als heute. Doch diese Zirkulation wird unterbrochen von Diskontinuitäten – welche hier zum Agitationsfeld der Künstlerin werden. Fari Shams stellt die Fülle der Bilder und die sich stets in ihr selbst überblendende Autorschaft in einen neuen, diskursiven Verhandlungsraum mit archäologisch-konzeptuellem Ansatz: durch Zusammenschlüsse zeigt sie die Bruchkanten, mittels absoluter Perfektion das Unvollständige, das Poröse, durch Exaktheit das Absurde. Ja, sie spielt mit den Mitteln der von ihr verwendeten Systeme – gegen den Apparat. ●

1 – Geoffrey Batchen, *Each Wild Idea: Writing, Photography, History* (Cambridge: MIT Press, 2002), S. 23.
2 – Baustelle Schaustelle, Essen (12. April—10. Mai 2013).
3 – Ausdruck von Gertrud Koch in Bezug darauf, „[...] dass Fotografie nicht notwendig referenziell sein muss, sondern in der Digitalisierung einen Zugewinn an Gestaltungsfreiheit und apparativer Autonomie gewinnen kann", in ihrem Text 'Tun oder so tun als ob? – alternative Strategien des Filmischen', in: Gertrud Koch und Christiane Voss (Hg.), *Es ist, als ob – Fiktionalität in Philosophie, Film- und Medienwissenschaft* (München: Fink 2009), S. 139.
4 – vgl. Vilém Flusser, *Für eine Philosophie der Fotografie* (Berlin: European Photography, 2011), S. 71. [erste Auflage 1983]
5 – Flusser 2011, S. 73.
6 – Batchen 2002, IX.
7 – ebd.
8 – vgl. hierzu Michael Hagners Überlegungen zu Fotobuch und Heterotopie: „Das Buch stellt einen Gegenraum zum Netz dar, das dessen Elemente aufnimmt, verarbeitet und transformiert, sich gegenüber dem Digitalen öffnet und wieder verschließt, das vermeintlich Unvereinbare zusammenführt. So wie Foucaults Heterotopien nicht unendlich große, sondern eng begrenzte Räume sind – zum Beispiel Gärten, Dachböden, Indianerzelte oder Schiffe –, so stellt auch das Buch einen begrenzten Raum dar." Michael Hagner, 'Das Fotobuch, postdigital', in: *Texte zur Kunst – Photography*, 99 (September 2015), S. 117.
9 – vgl. Flusser 2011, S. 34.
10 – vgl. Herta Wolf, 'Positivismus, Historismus, Fotografie – Zu verschiedenen Aspekten der Gleichsetzung von Geschichte und Fotografie', in: *Fotografiegeschichte*, 63, Jg. 17 (1997), S. 36.
11 – ebd., S. 38.
12 – „Bild gegen Bild" entlehnt dem Titel: *Bild gegen Bild – Image Counter Image*, Ausstellungskatalog anlässlich der gleichnamigen Ausstellung und Konferenz im Haus der Kunst München (Köln: Walther König, 2012).
13 – „Es handelte sich damals [im 18. Jahrhundert] darum, die Natur durch eine konstante Tafel der Identitäten und der Unterschiede aufzuteilen, für die die Sprache einen ersten, annähernden und korrigierbaren Raster lieferte. Jetzt ist die Sprache Bild [...]", Michel Foucault, *Die Ordnung der Dinge* (Frankfurt am Main: Suhrkamp, 1971), S. 361.
14 – Susan Sontag, *Das Leiden Anderer betrachten*, (München/Wien: Hanser, 2003), S. 55-56.
15 - Judith Butler, 'Folter und die Ethik der Fotografie', in: Linda Hentschel (Hg.), *Bilderpolitik* (Berlin: bbooks, 2008), S. 207.
16 – Peter Osborne, 'Das verteilte Bild', in: *Texte zur Kunst – Photography*, 99 (September 2015), S. 81.
17 – Hans-Peter Feldmann im Gespräch mit Kasper König, in: Helena Taty (Hg.), Feldmann, Hans-Peter: *Another Book*, Ausstellungskatalog (London: Koenig, 2010), Extrabeilage S. 11. Das Interview wurde erstmals veröffentlicht in: *Frieze Magazine*, Mai 2005.
18 – vgl. Michael Hagner, 'Das Fotobuch, postdigital', in: *Texte zur Kunst – Photography*, 99 (September 2015), S. 115.
19 – Batchen 2002, S. 129.
20 – vgl. Susan Buck-Morss, „The temporal matrix in which truth is embedded, essentially transient, is the criterion for critical judgment – a difficult idea, because it goes against conventional procedures that narrate history sequentially and at a distance. In view of the fleeting nature of truth, any attempt at permanence of historical interpretation leads to error. [...] Past events cannot provide a key to the present unless they are radically separated from a direct lineage of inheritance." Susan Buck-Morss, 'The Gift of the Past, Constellations', in: documenta 13 – *Das Buch der Bücher* (Ostfildern: Hatje Cantz, 2012), S. 96/97.
21 – Batchen 2002, IX.
22 – Buck-Morss (ebd.), S. 94.
23 – „[...] Poetry leads to the same place. Blending and fusion of separate objects. It leads us to death and through death to continuity. Photographs have layed down these routes [sic!]. Made out of dung. Created by ideologies. Archives of images, representative images, which encapsulate common ideas of significance. Not piles but poster-ready pools. Oceans. The Sun matched with the Sea." Arranged by Geoffrey Farmer, in: Tobias Spichtig und Fabian Schöneich (Hg.), *Blue, Red, and Green* (Berlin: Sternberg Press, 2012), S. 6. Siehe hierzu auch Geoffrey Farmers Auseinandersetzung mit fotografischen Ideologien am Beispiel LIFE in seiner Arbeit ‚Leaves of Grass' (2012).

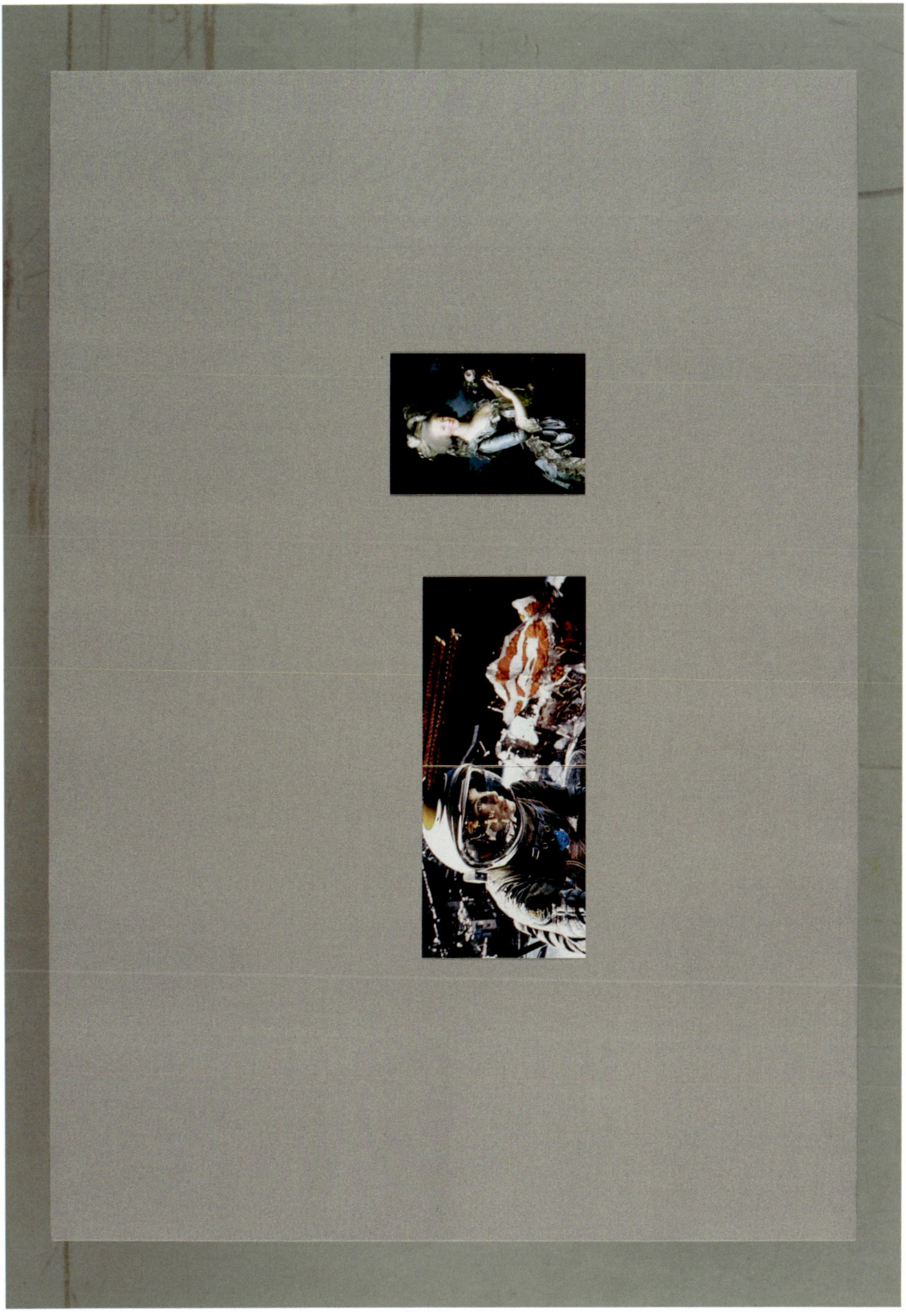

hats (plate 3) MA

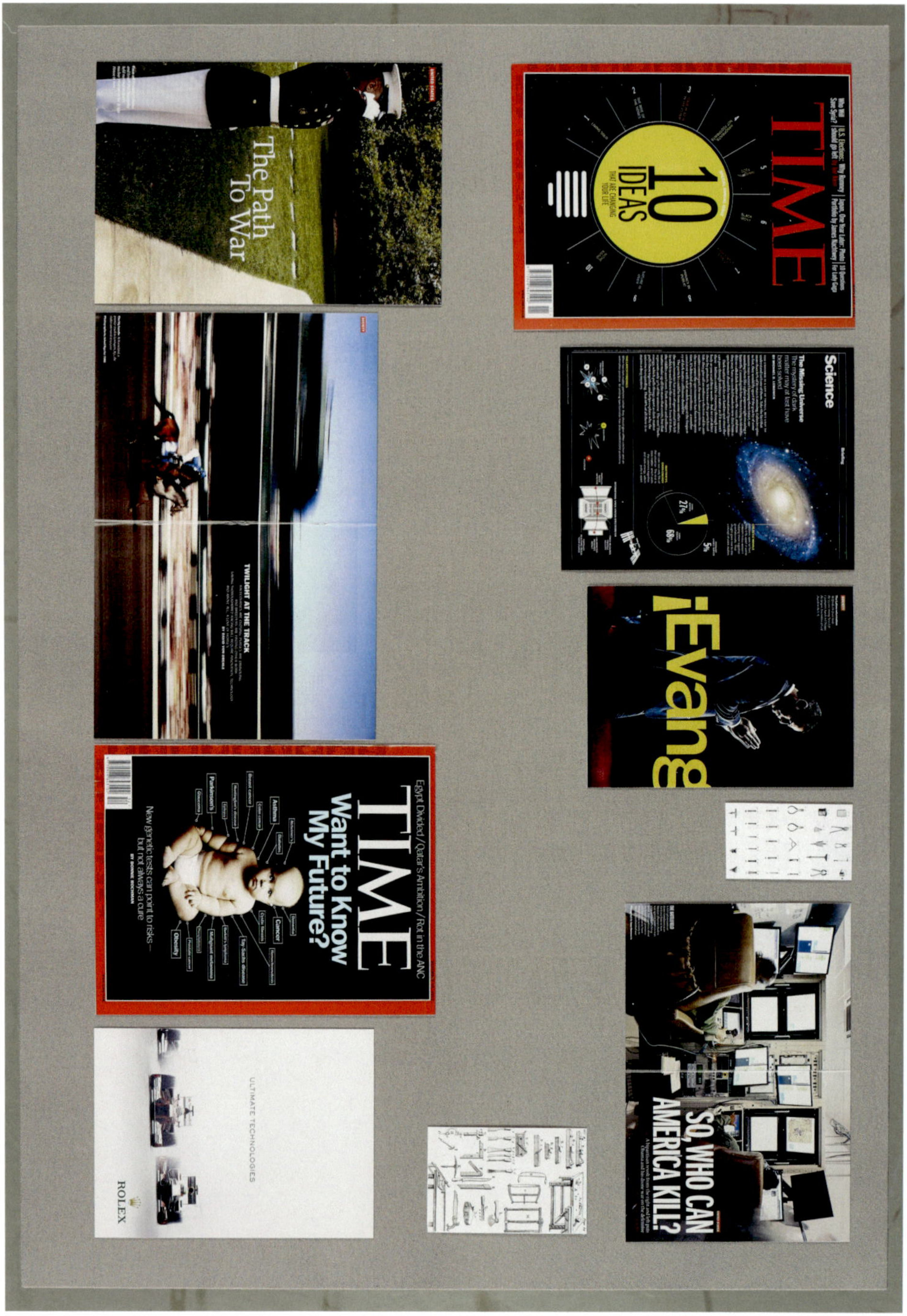
The Path To War
TIME
10 IDEAS THAT ARE CHANGING YOUR LIFE
Science
The Missing Universe
TWILIGHT AT THE TRACK
¡Evang
Egypt Divided / Qatar's Ambition / Rot in the ANC
TIME
Want to Know My Future?
New genetic tests can point to risks — but not always a cure
SO, WHO CAN AMERICA KILL?
ULTIMATE TECHNOLOGIES
ROLEX

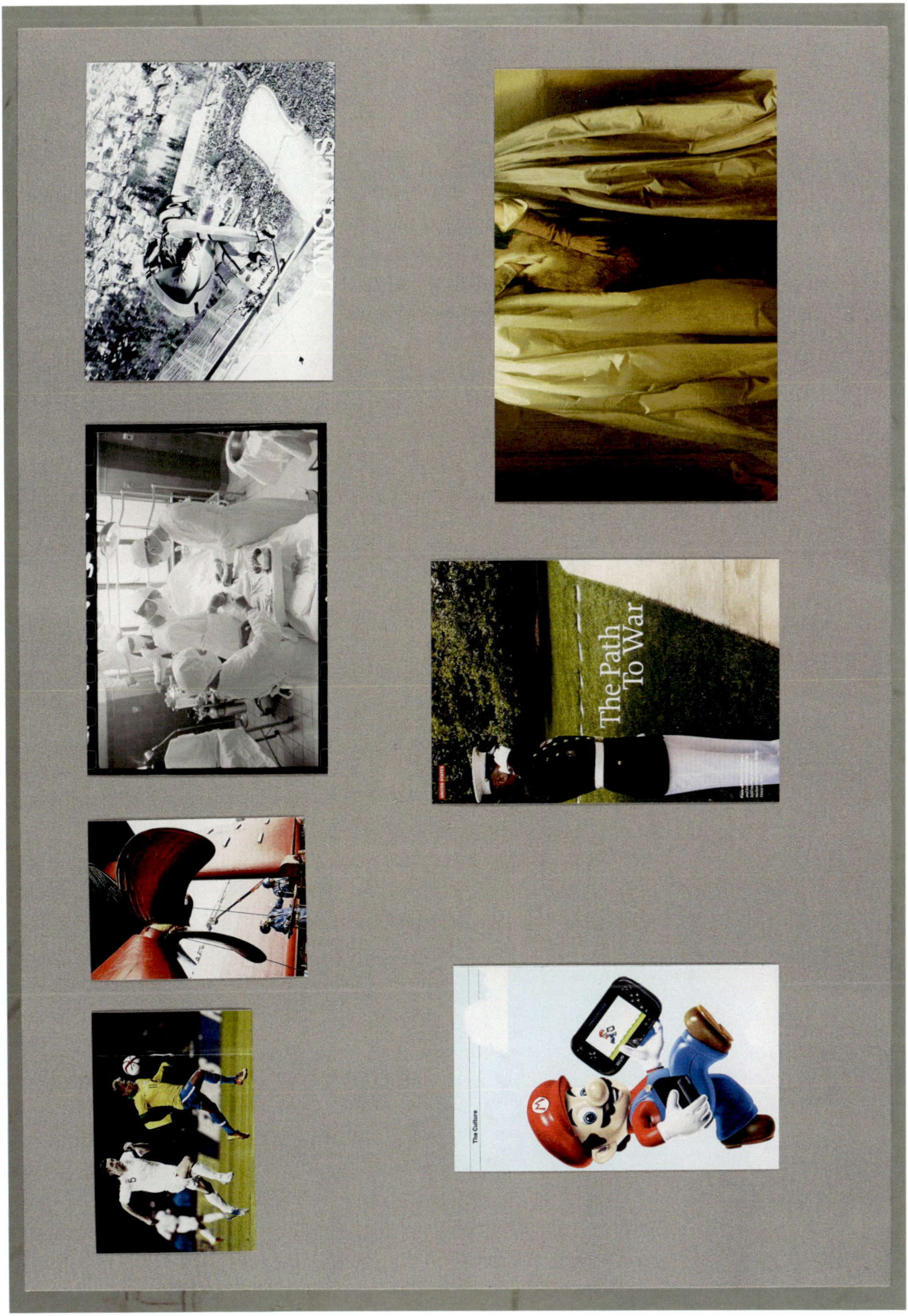
The Path
To War

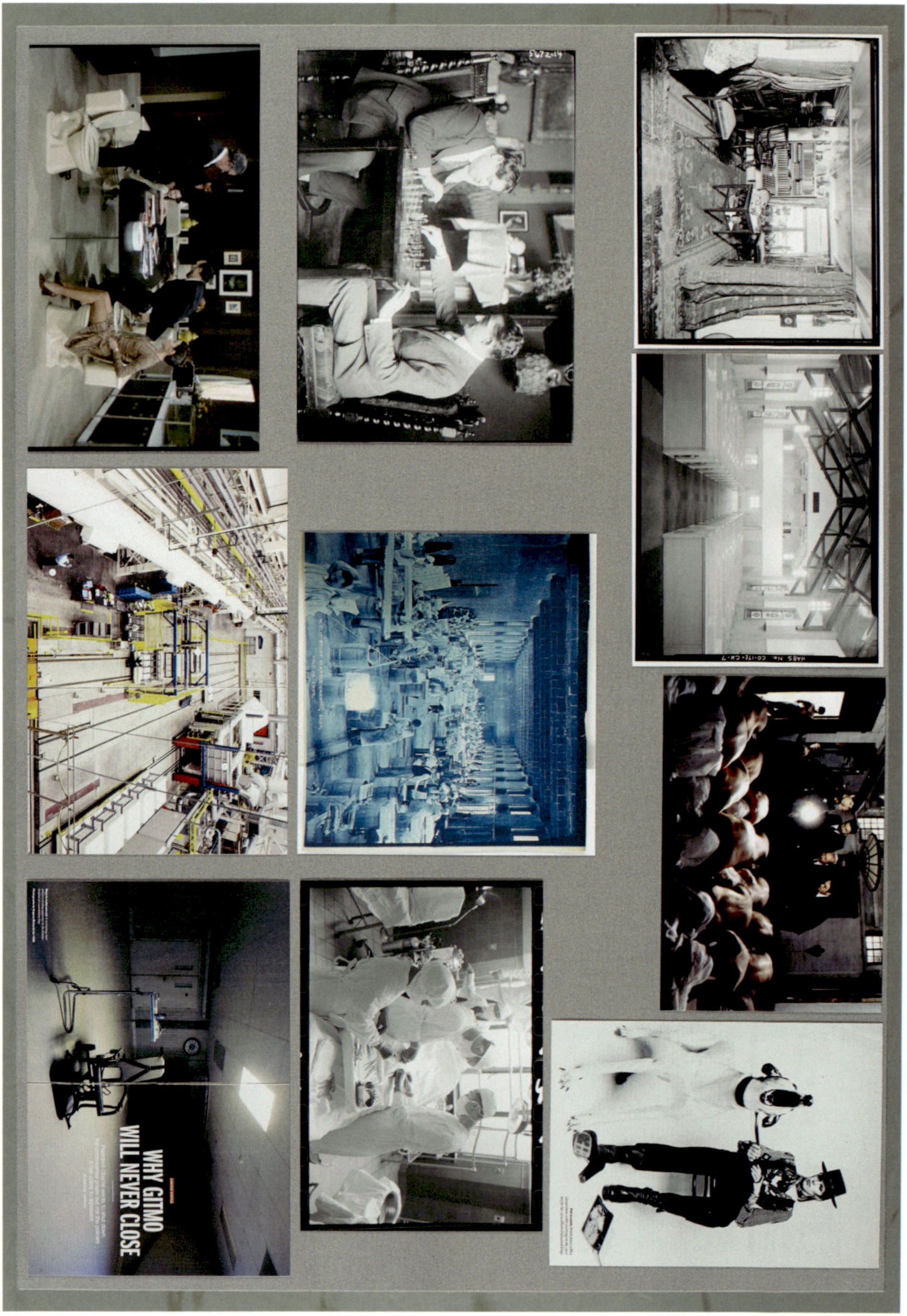

interior (plate 4) MA

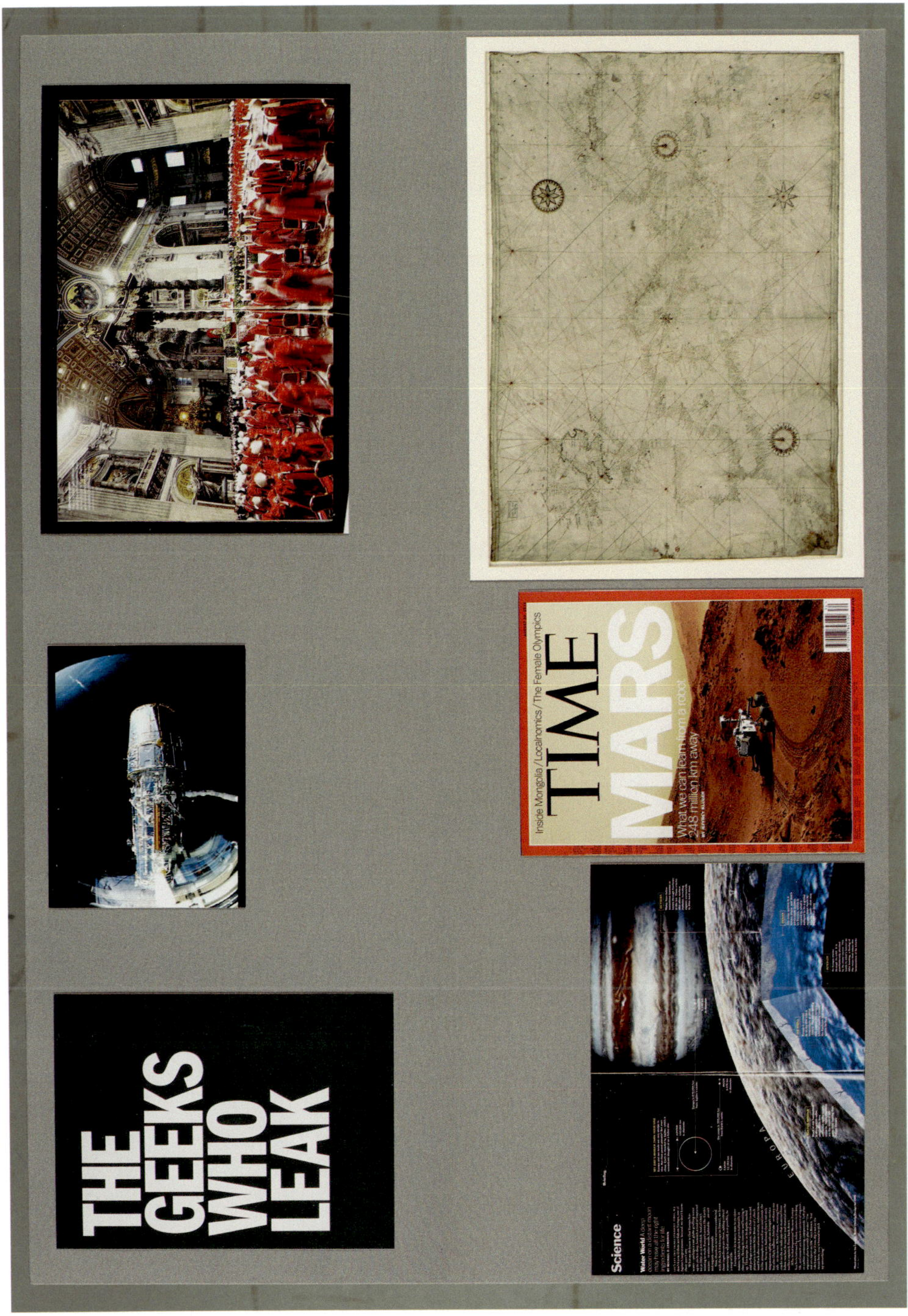
THE GEEKS WHO LEAK
Inside Mongolia / Localnomics / The Female Olympics
TIME
MARS
What we can learn from a robot 248 million km away
Science

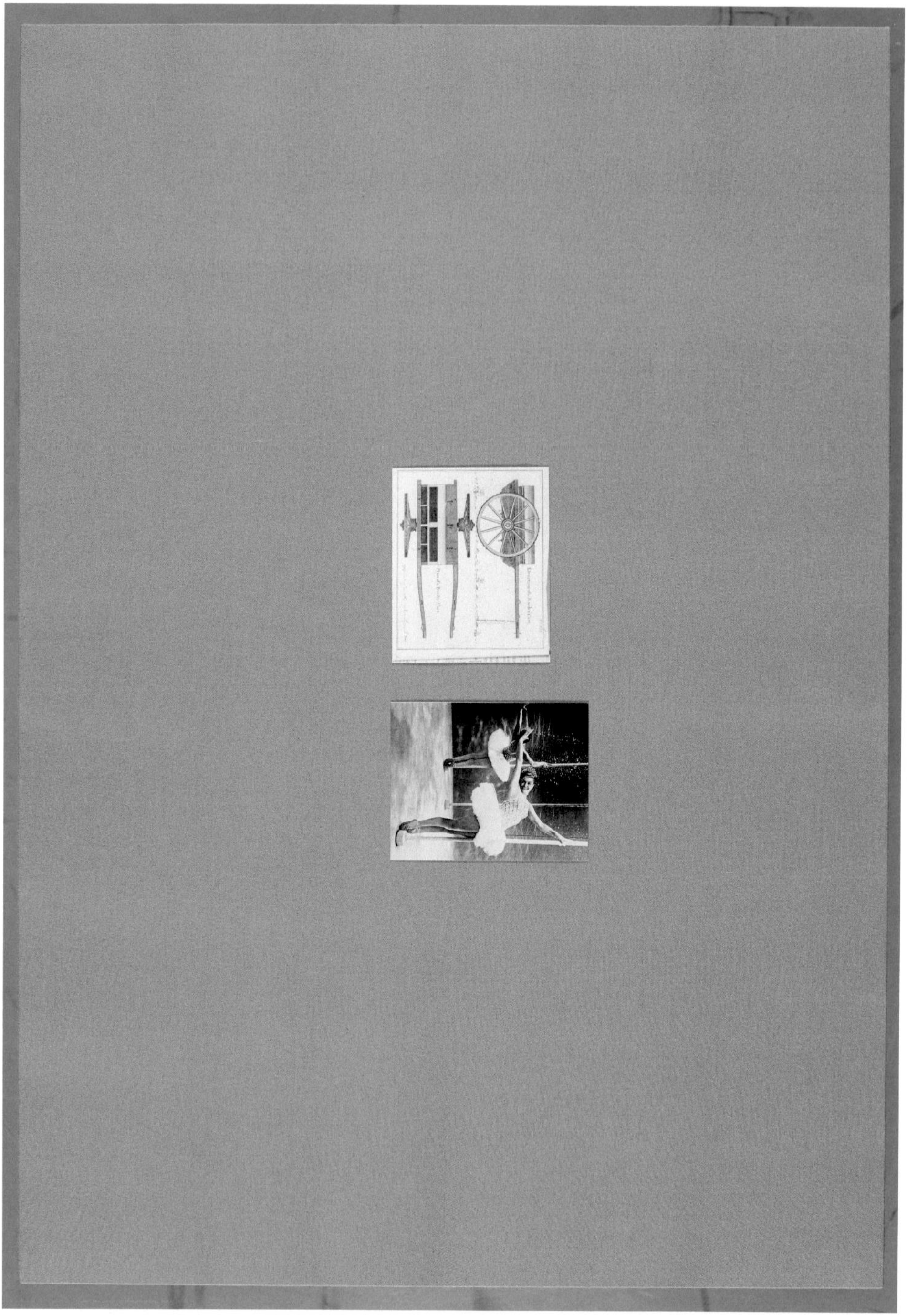

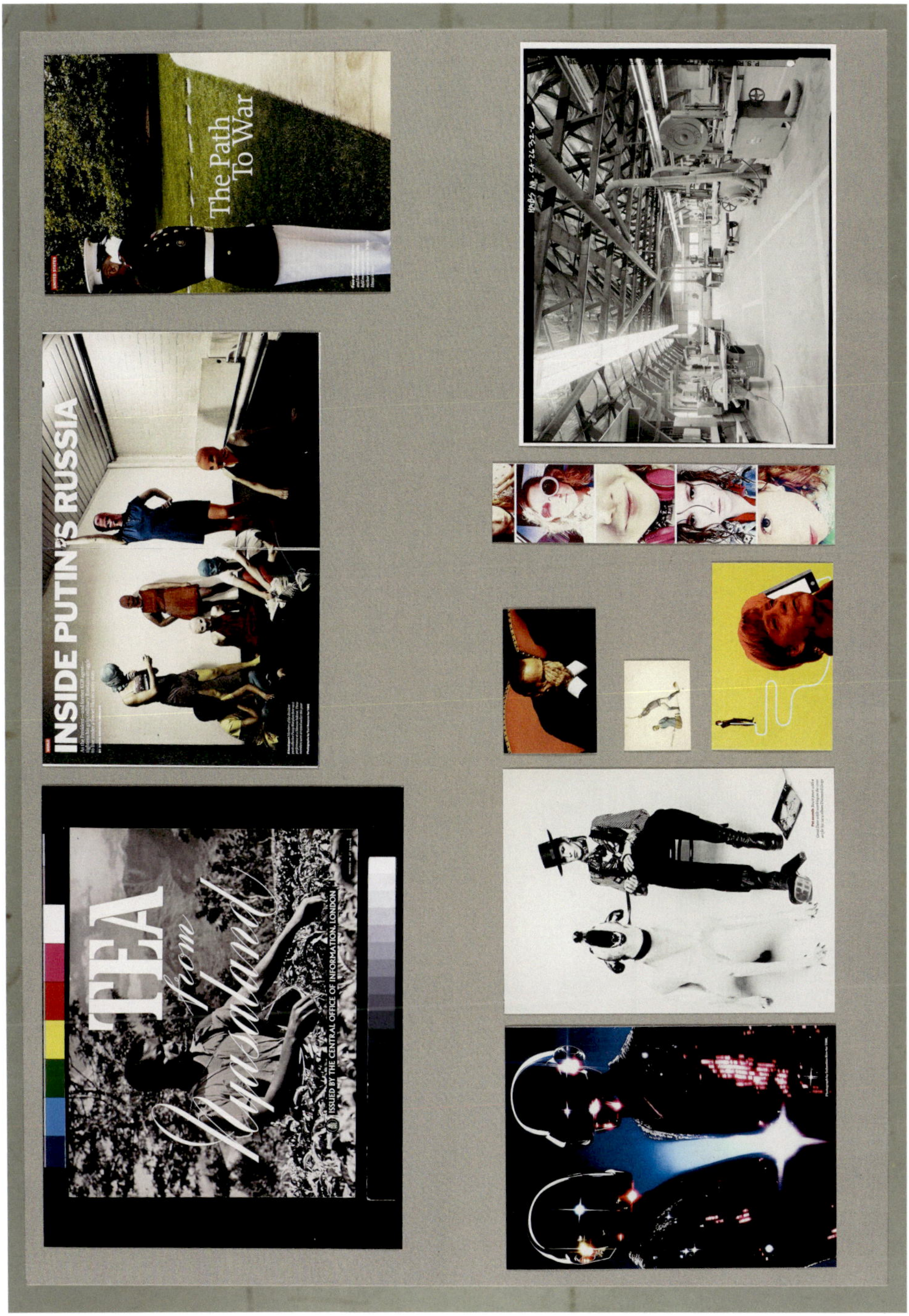
The Path To War
INSIDE PUTIN'S RUSSIA
TEA from Nyasaland
ISSUED BY THE CENTRAL OFFICE OF INFORMATION, LONDON

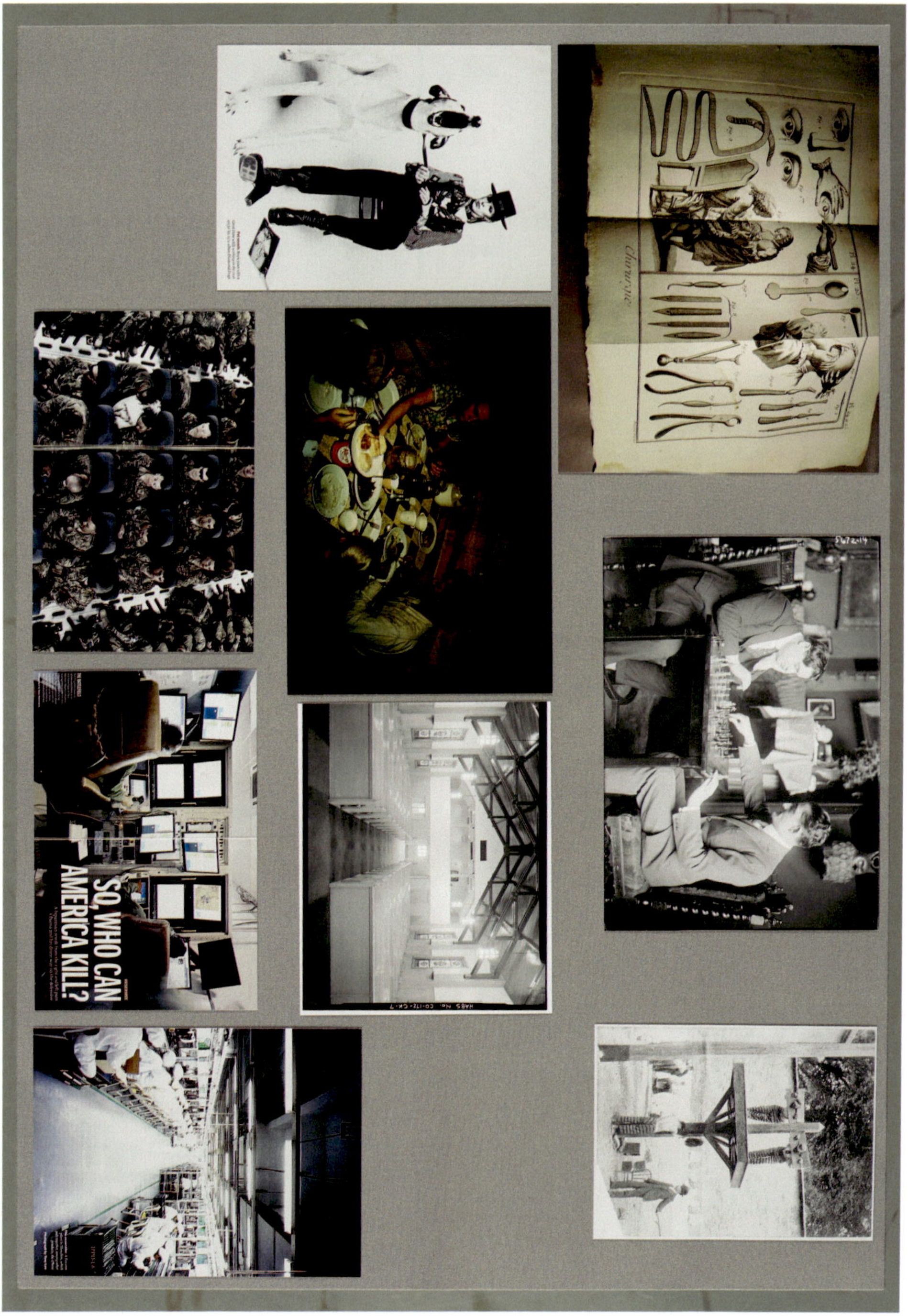
SO, WHO CAN AMERICA KILL?

Daniela Stöppel

PETER DER GROSSE UND DIE ORDNUNG SEINER WELT

Mit dem Projekttitel *European Civilization Peter the Great and the Order of Things* bezieht sich Fari Shams nicht nur explizit auf Michel Foucaults Abhandlung *Les mots et les choses* (1966), sondern auch auf den russischen Zar Peter den Großen (1672–1725), der mit seinen Reformen das russische Reich nach westlichen Vorbildern modernisierte und ab 1703 mithilfe ausländischer Baumeister Sankt Petersburg aus dem Boden stampfen ließ. Die Neuordnung des Zarenreichs unter seiner Regentschaft spiegelte sich in einer Rechtschreibreform, der Einrichtung systematisch aufgebauter Kunst- und Naturkundesammlungen, einer Alphabetisierungskampagne und anderen Großprojekten wider. Mit Peter dem Großen beschäftigt sich Fari Shams intensiver seit einer Russland-Reise 2013.

Besonders anschaulich lassen sich die Petrinischen Reformbestrebungen in Sankt Petersburg und seiner städtebaulichen Ordnung nachvollziehen. Diese beschrieb der russische Symbolist Andrej Belyj in seinem 1905 verfassten Roman *Petersburg* als von der geraden Achse des Newskij-Prospekts bestimmt: „Petersburg als Ganzes ist die Unendlichkeit des Prospekts, in die Potenz n erhoben.“[1] Auch die „Linien“, wie die parallel verlaufenden Straßen der Wassilewskij-Insel bis heute genannt werden, bewahrten „die Erinnerung an das alte Petersburg, die Stadt Peters.“[2]

Einer der Protagonisten des Romans, der hohe Staatsbeamte Apollon Apollonowitsch, dem schon aus professionellen Gründen an der richtigen Ordnung der Welt wesentlich gelegen ist, verspürt während einer Kutschfahrt das starke Verlangen, dass „ein Prospekt nach dem anderen, daß Reihen schwarzgrauer Häuserwürfel gleich Schlangenwindungen die ganze Kugeloberfläche des Planeten umspannten, daß die ganze von Prospekten umschlossene Erde in linearem kosmischen Lauf die Unendlichkeit nach dem Gesetz der geraden Linie durchschneide; daß das Netz von parallelen Prospekten, von einem zweiten Netz paralleler Prospekte geschnitten, sich als System von Quadraten und Würfeln über alle Abgründe des Weltalls dehnte [...].“[3]

Das quadratische Raster soll sich also, ausgehend vom Newskij-Prospekt, als Netz von Planquadraten über die gesamte Welt ausdehnen. Die Romanfigur des Verwaltungsbeamten Apollon Apollonowitsch führt damit die von Peter dem Großen begonnene Ordnung Petersburg als Weltordnung fort. Der Name Apollon Apollonowitsch ist als Gegensatz zum Dionysischen zu verstehen, und schon 1902 bezeichnete der Symbolist Alexander Benois Sankt Petersburg als „apollinisch“, da es den „Geist der Ordnung, den Geist der vollendeten Formen des Lebens“ verkörpere und „die allgemeine Schlamperei“ nicht hinnehme. Apollonowitsch wendet diesen Geist der Ordnung, wie Belyj uns wissen lässt, sogar im eigenen häuslichen Umfeld an:
„Apollon Apollonowitsch hatte sich nur ein einziges Mal um die kleinen Dinge des Lebens gekümmert: er hatte das häusliche Inventar revidiert, ordnungsgemäß registriert und

sämtliche großen und kleinen Fächer mit Buchstaben versehen. Die Fächer waren mit den Buchstaben a, b und c bezeichnet, ihre vier Seiten nach den Himmelsrichtungen benannt. Als Apollon Apollonowitsch seine Brille weglegte, hatte er in seiner kleinen, minutiösen Schrift in sein Verzeichnis eingetragen: Brille – Fach b, NO, das heißt Nord-Ost, und seinem Kammerdiener eine Kopie der Liste gegeben."[4]

Das kartographische, rektolineare Koordinatensystem des Stadtgrundrisses hält auf diese Weise Einzug in Apollon Apollonowitschs Haushaltsführung, in der sich so die von Peter dem Großen eingeführte Ordnungslogik als Mikrostruktur fortsetzt.

Die aus dem Geist des Absolutismus geborene Bürokratie des russischen Zarentums, die sich in der Beamten- und Soldatenstadt Sankt Petersburg architektonisch verfestigt hat, gerät jedoch durch die Revolution von 1905, von der Belyjs Roman im Weiteren handelt, ins Wanken. Bei Belyj manifestiert sich dieser Umsturz im literarischen Zusammenprall des Rastersystems mit amorphen, formlosen Strukturen; damit verleiht er nicht nur der Instabilität der neuen Weltordnung Ausdruck, sondern lässt zugleich in den entstehenden Rissen im Raumkontinuum eine neue, utopisch-geistige Dimension aufscheinen. Diese entfaltet sich schattenhaft in den nichteuklidischen Zwischenräumen: Die formlose Gestalt der neuen anarchistischen Bewegungen öffnet gleichsam den Spalt zu einer neuen Welt – hinter allen Ordnungen. Mithin denkt Belyj seine Revolution weniger als Neuordnung der Welt, sondern als Aufhebung von Ordnung. Dies sei hier, wo es um Europäische Zivilisationen im Allgemeinen geht, als Perspektive zumindest angedeutet. Auf das Prinzip der Unordnung oder Nicht-Ordnung jedenfalls wird noch zurückzukommen sein.

Wie die meisten Systeme ist auch Sankt Petersburg ein abstraktes Gebilde, eine Schöpfung aus dem Nichts, eine apriorische Setzung, eine Kopfgeburt. Die Linie des Newskij-Prospekt wurde als Gerade von der Admiralität bis zum Alexander-Newski-Kloster gezogen. Als artifizielle Perspektive (ein weiterer Name für die Straßen Petersburgs) definiert sie das weitere Koordinatensystem als Macht- und Repräsentationsraum.

Während die großen Ordnungssysteme der französischen Klassik bis hin zu Diderots und d'Alemberts *Enzyklopädie* (ab 1751) bis heute als Werke der Aufklärung gelten können, fällt dies bei den Projekten Peters schwer. Zu sehr erweisen sich seine Reformbemühungen als mit Gewalt durch(ge)setzt, als Herrschaftsinstrumente, um politische Macht nicht nur zu stabilisieren, sondern auch auszudehnen. So war es nur deshalb möglich, Sankt Petersburg aus den finnischen Sümpfen zu stampfen, weil auf der Grundlage des Ukas die leibeigene Bevölkerung zu Fronarbeit und Zusatzsteuern gezwungen werden konnte. Gerade an den Reformen Peters des Großen wird also die grundsätzliche Zwiespältigkeit der Aufklärung anschaulich, denn diese richtet sich nicht per se gegen Alleinherrschaft und autoritäre Machtausübung, sondern formiert ein eigenes Machtsystem. So besteht zwischen Aufklärung und Willkür nur ein scheinbarer Gegensatz: Im Grunde sind sie die zwei Seiten der gleichen Medaille.

Auch Fari Shams setzt an den Anfang ihres Projektes eine subjektive und damit auktoriale Geste: Ihren Bilder-Corpus von 145 Fotografien hat sie auf der Grundlage einer Vorlesung von John Merriman über Peter den Großen zusammengestellt. Dies ist eine subjektive Entscheidung, die dennoch – im Rückgriff auf eine standardisierte Überblicksvorlesung der Yale University – Allgemeingültigkeit beansprucht. Über Schlagwortsuchen wurden dann die Fotografien im *TIME* Magazine sowie in der Datenbank der Library of Congress ermittelt – auch hier setzt sich das Prinzip von subjektiver Entscheidung und allgemeingültiger Tragweite fort. In einem nächsten Schritt unterzog sie nun diesen Bilderkorpus verschiedenen Anordnungssystemen, denen teils anerkannte historische Bedeutung zukommt, wie Diderots *Système Figuré des Connaissances Humaines* oder Michel Adansons Methode der Artenklassizfizierung, die teils aber auch ganz persönlichen Entscheidungen unterliegen, wie die intuitive Gegenüberstellung von Bilderpaaren.

Damit setzt sie der Scheinobjektivität der Klassifikationssysteme jeweils subjektive Setzungen entgegen: Transparenz und Intransparenz der Methode vermischen sich. Die Parallelität ganz unterschiedlicher Anordnungsmuster betont deren Arbitrarität und erinnert an Momentaufnahmen eines sich permanent im Fluss befindenden Denkens. So zieht Fari Shams immer wieder neue Querschnitte, die sich jedoch letztlich gegenseitig aufheben.

Schon in der Auswahl von Diderot einerseits und Adanson andererseits spiegelt sich ihr Anliegen einer Dekonstruktion. So dienen ausgerechnet diese beiden Autoren Foucault in *Les mots et les choses* dazu, „System" und „Methode" voneinander abzugrenzen: Während Diderot auf Grundlage empirischer Datenerhebung ein System errichtet, anhand dessen alle weiter beobachtbaren Dinge klassifiziert werden können, vertritt Adanson eine strukturell offene und unabgeschlossene Klassifizierung, indem er neue Arten aufgrund der Unterschiede zu bereits bestimmten, i.e. beschriebenen Spezies definiert.

In Shams' Arbeit *European Civilization Peter the Great and the Order of Things* werden diese Methoden nun auf Bilder übertragen, was einer Art Feldversuch gleichkommt: Welche Anordnungen ergeben sich nach Diderots Schema, und wie sehen die Gruppen aus, die nach Adansons Methode zustande kommen? Wie unterscheiden sich Ordnungen nach Begriffsmerkmalen von denen nach Formmerkmalen?

Die erste Ordnung folgt einer alphabetischen Ordnung. Dazu müssen den Dingen (*choses*) Wörter (*mots*) an die Seite gestellt werden, die hier zumeist mit dem Titel des Bildes identisch sind. Bekanntermaßen ist das Verhältnis zwischen Dingen und Wörtern in der Regel arbiträr, so dass auch bei Shams eine – aus inhaltlicher und formaler Perspektive – zufällige Anordnung entsteht. So finden sich unter dem Buchstaben G: „41. Games, 42. Garden, 43. Golden boy und 44. Griffith observatory LA" – also Bezeichnungen, die weder inhaltlich noch formal in irgendeinem engeren Zusammenhang stehen. Auch die zugeordneten Bilder (von Super-Mario, einem Landschaftsgarten, einem Zweikampf zwischen Fußballern und einem Observatorium) haben nichts gemeinsam (siehe Seite 77).

Das zweite Ordnungssystem orientiert sich an Diderots *Système Figuré des Connaissances Humaines*. Auch hier geht es um ein Verhältnis zwischen Dingen (oder beobachtbaren Phänomenen) und Begriffen. Indem Diderot sämtliche Erscheinungen, die er ordnen will, in sein begriffliches Klassifikationssystem einpasst, abstrahiert er zwar von den (Eigen-)Namen der Dinge, überträgt jedoch begriffliche Kategorienbildung auf die vielfältigen Erscheinungen des

Lebens. Fari Shams vollzieht Diderots Dreiteilung in *Mémoire, Raison, Imagination* an ihrem Bild-Corpus nach und ordnet beispielsweise ein Observatorium der Kategorie *Vernunft* zu. Sie überträgt also die bei Diderot klassifizierten Begriffe auf aktuelle fotografische Reproduktionen, was unter anderem die Historizität seines apriorischen Systems deutlich macht. Der Akt des Zuordnens selbst erscheint auf diese Weise nicht völlig trennbar von subjektiven Entscheidungen.

Anders als bei der alphabetischen Ordnung lassen sich nun aber durchaus formale Übereinstimmungen bei gleich zugeordneten Bildern feststellen. Bestimmte geometrische Formen scheinen dem Rationalen also eher zu entsprechen, als der *Imagination*. Das Raster, das Belyj in seinem Roman beschreibt, taucht beispielsweise des Öfteren unter *Vernunft* auf. Peters Straßensystem kehrt hier gleichsam wiedergängerisch in Form des Rasters einer Vermessung eines menschlichen Körpers zurück. Und auch das genannte Observatorium befindet sich nun in Gesellschaft mit anderen Kreis- und Kuppelformationen (siehe Seite 78).

Bei Michel Adanson schließlich wird anstelle eines übergeordneten Systems eine Methode des Ordnens präsentiert, die über formale Vergleichung Bild-Gruppen entstehen lässt. Shams vollzieht diese Methode, indem sie die Bilder in der Reihenfolge der arbiträren alphabetischen Ordnung beschreibt, Stichworte identifiziert und über diese Stichworte dann die Bilder zu Gruppen zusammenführt. Zentral an der Methode Adansons ist dabei, dass nur die Abweichungen beschrieben werden. So wird beispielsweise die Gruppe „round dominant shapes" gebildet, die sich interessanterweise wieder nicht nur formal ausgrenzen lässt, sondern auch inhaltliche Bezüge schafft. Das Observatorium wird nun von einer Krebszelle, einer Kirche, einem gestreiften Overall und anderem begleitet, das Rückschlüsse auf bestimmte Form-Inhalt-Relationen zulässt (siehe Seite 79).

Shams nähert sich so von verschiedenen Seiten der Fragestellung an, inwiefern Form und Inhalt miteinander korrespondieren und welche historischen Antworten darauf gefunden wurden.

Im persönlichen Zugriff auf das Material schließlich sowie in der tautologischen Gesamtkonstruktion des Projekts wird jedoch die Möglichkeit nach allgemeingültiger Ordnung grundsätzlich in Frage gestellt. Die Machtfrage ist also in der Pluralität der Ansätze nicht aufgehoben, sondern wird dadurch nur umso deutlicher sichtbar. Ein Ausstieg aus dieser immer wieder neu zu vollziehenden Ordnung der Welt scheint nicht möglich zu sein.

Abschließend kann aber – unter Bezugnahme auf Daniil Charms Text *Traktat mehr oder weniger nach der Lektüre Emersons* (1939) – eine Aufhebung von jeglicher Ordnung zumindest als utopisches Ziel angedeutet werden. Dort heißt es zur Hierarchie der Dinge am Beispiel des Schenkens:

> *Unvollkommene Geschenke sind solche Geschenke: zum Beispiel: wir schenken jemandem zum Namenstag den Deckel eines Tintenfasses. Und wo ist das Tintenfaß selbst? Oder wir schenken ihm ein Tintenfaß mit Deckel. Und wo ist der Tisch, auf dem das Tintenfaß stehen sollte? Wenn der Beschenkte schon einen Tisch hat, so wird das*

Tintenfaß zum vollkommenen Geschenk. Stets vollkommene Geschenke sind Schmuckstücke für den nackten Körper, wie zum Beispiel Ringe, Armreifen, Colliers usw. [...], oder Geschenke wie, zum Beispiel, ein Stäbchen, an dessen einem Ende eine kleine Holzkugel befestigt ist, am anderen Ende dagegen ein hölzerner Würfel. Ein solches Stäbchen kann man in Händen halten oder, wenn man es weglegt, dann ist vollkommen gleichgültig, wohin. Ein solches Stäbchen ist sonst zu nichts nütze.[5]

Ein apollinisches Koordinatensystem oder auch die vergleichende Methode Adansons erwiesen sich als auf ein Holzstäbchen mit Kugel- und Würfel-Anhängseln schlicht als nicht anwendbar. So könnte ein Hinwegsetzen über Ordnungen auf der Grundlage eines anderen Objekt-Subjekt-Verhältnisses geschehen. Eine Idee, die, wie Shams uns zeigt, sich möglicherweise auch auf visuelles Material wie fotografische Reproduktionen anwenden ließe. ●

1 – Andrey Belyj, *Petersburg* (München: DTV, 1962) [Erstveröffentlichung 1913, verfasst 1905], S. 17.

2 – Ebd., S. 18

3 – Ebd., S. 16.

4 – Ebd., S. 10.

5 – Daniil Charms, 'Traktat mehr oder weniger nach der Lektüre Emersons' [1939], zit. n. Boris Groys / Aage Hansen-Löve (Hg.), *Am Nullpunkt. Positionen der russischen Avantgarde* (Frankfurt am Main: 2005), S. 651-565.

MICHEL ADANSON'S SYSTEM OF CLASSIFICATION OF PLANTS IN SENEGAL DESCRIBED BY MICHEL FOUCAULT

Instead of selecting, from the totality described, the element — whether few or numerous — that are to be used as characters, the method consists in deducing them stage by stage. One begins — as Adanson did in his examination of the plants of Senegal[1]. One describes it in its entirety, leaving out none of its parts and determining all the values that the variables have derived from it. This process is repeated with the next species, also given by the arbitrary nature of representation. The description should be as total as in the first instance, but with the one difference that nothing that has been mentioned in the first description should be repeated in the second. Only the differences are listed. And similarly with the third species in relation to the first two, and so on indefinitely. So that, at the very end, all the different features of all the plants have been listed once, but never more than once. And by arranging the latter and progressively more sparse descriptions around the earlier ones, we shall be able to perceive, through the original chaos, the emergence of the general table of relations[2].

1 – Michel Adanson, *Histoire naturelle du Senegal* (Paris: 1757).

2 – Michel Foucault, *The Order of Things. An Archaeology of the Human Sciences.* (New York: Pantheon Books, 1971).

MAP OF THE SYSTEM
of HUMAN KNOWLEDGE

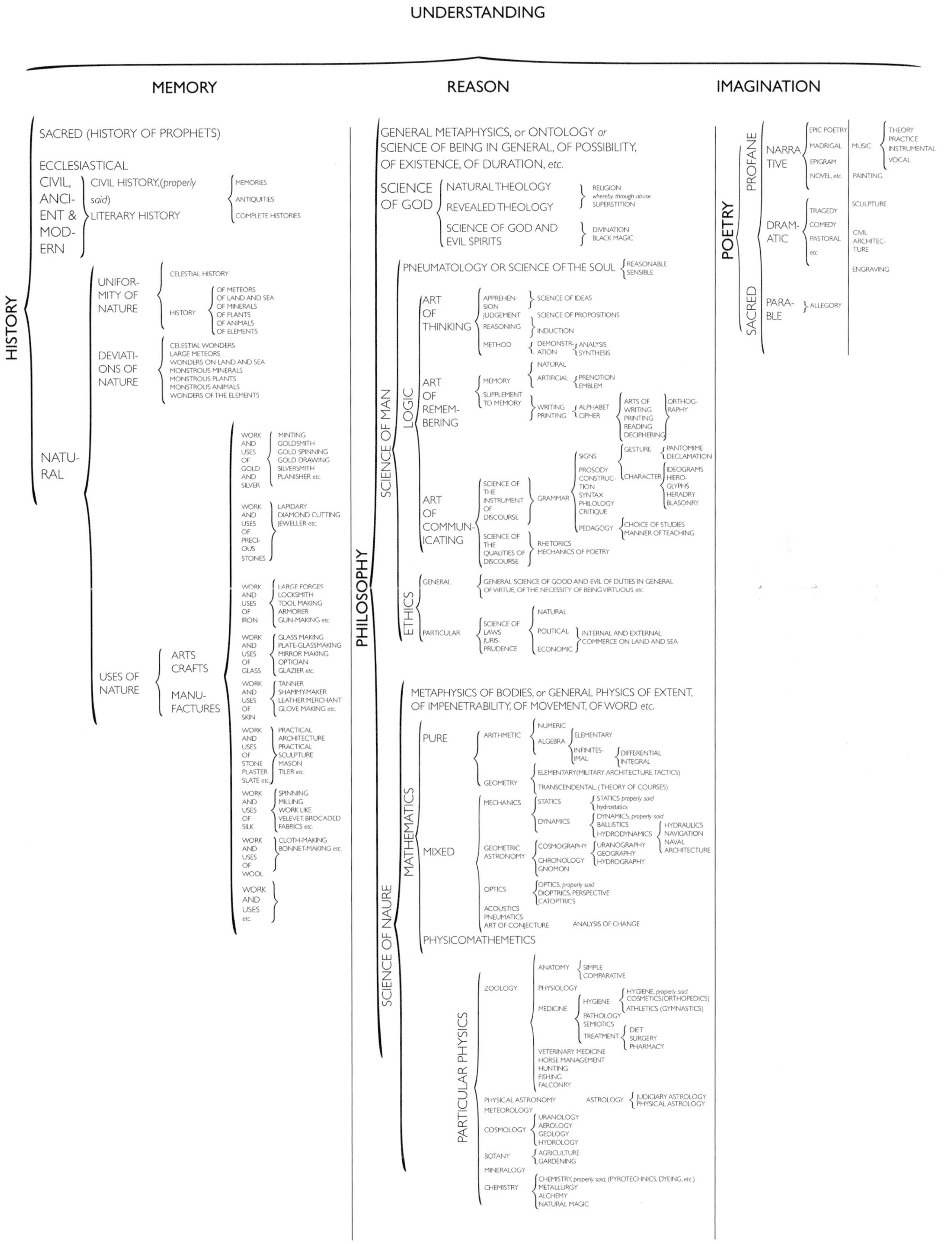

MAP OF THE SYSTEM
of HUMAN KNOWLEDGE

UNDERSTANDING

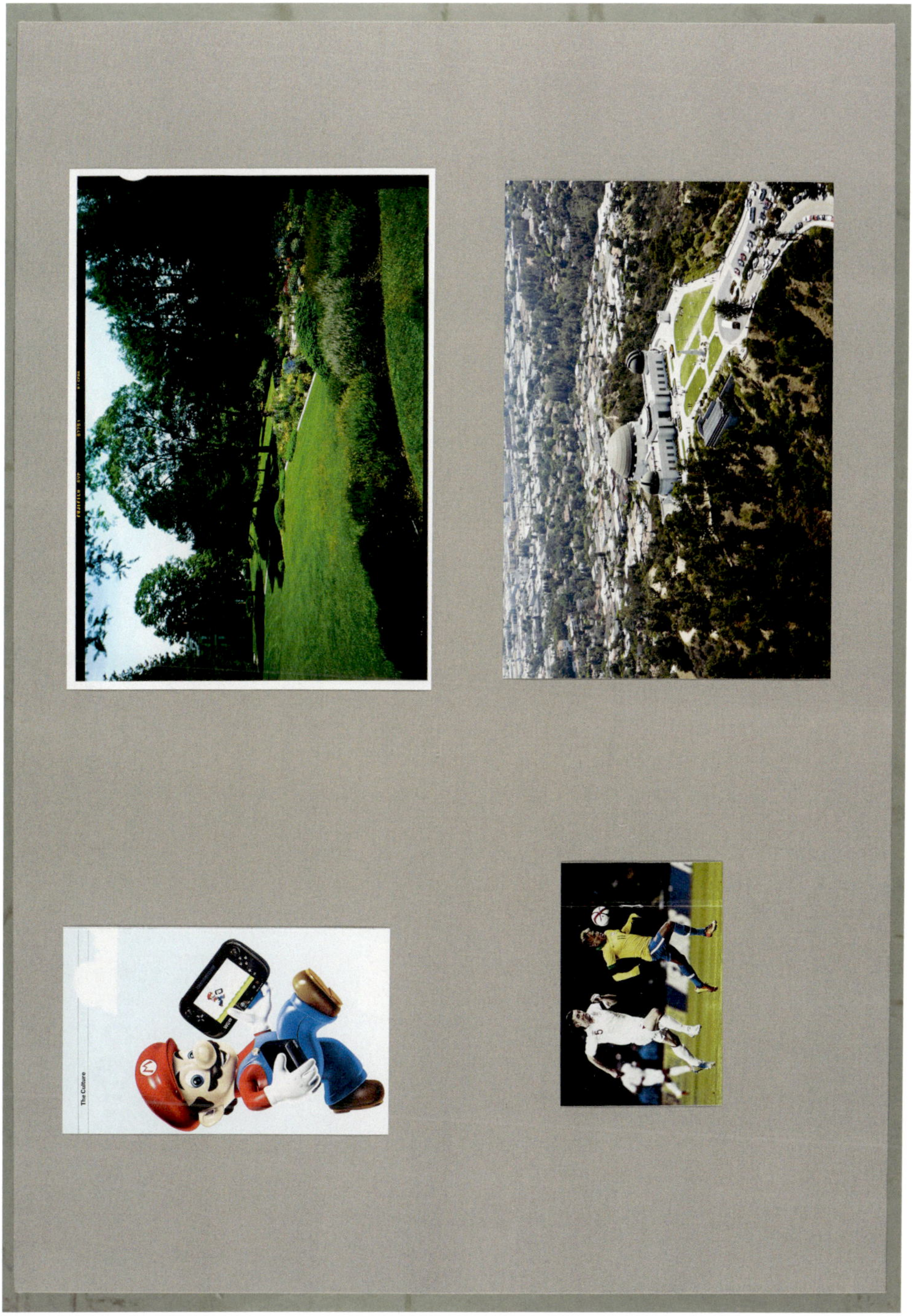
The Culture

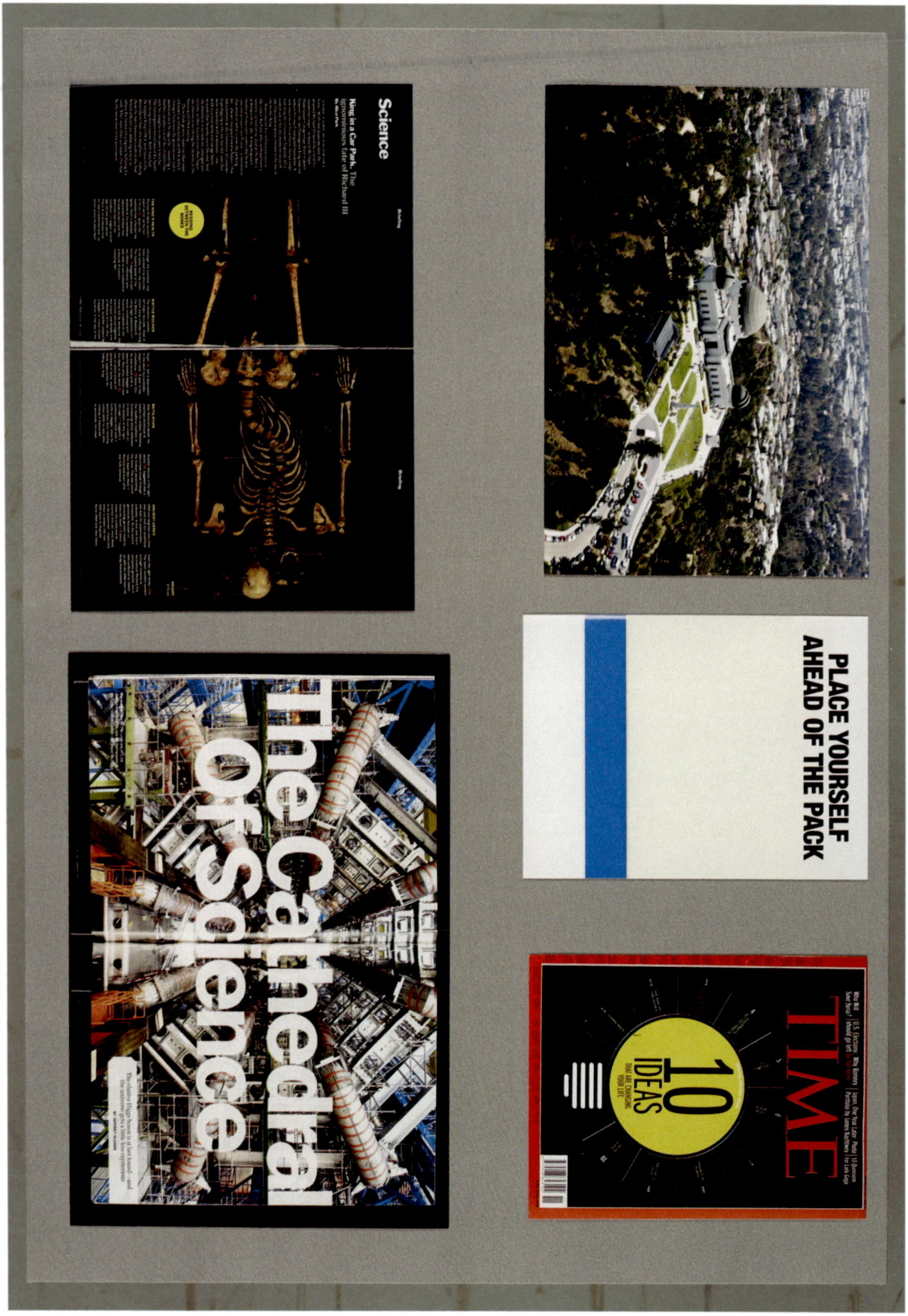
Science
King in a Car Park. The ignominious fate of Richard III
PLACE YOURSELF AHEAD OF THE PACK
The Cathedral Of Science
TIME
10 IDEAS THAT ARE CHANGING YOUR LIFE

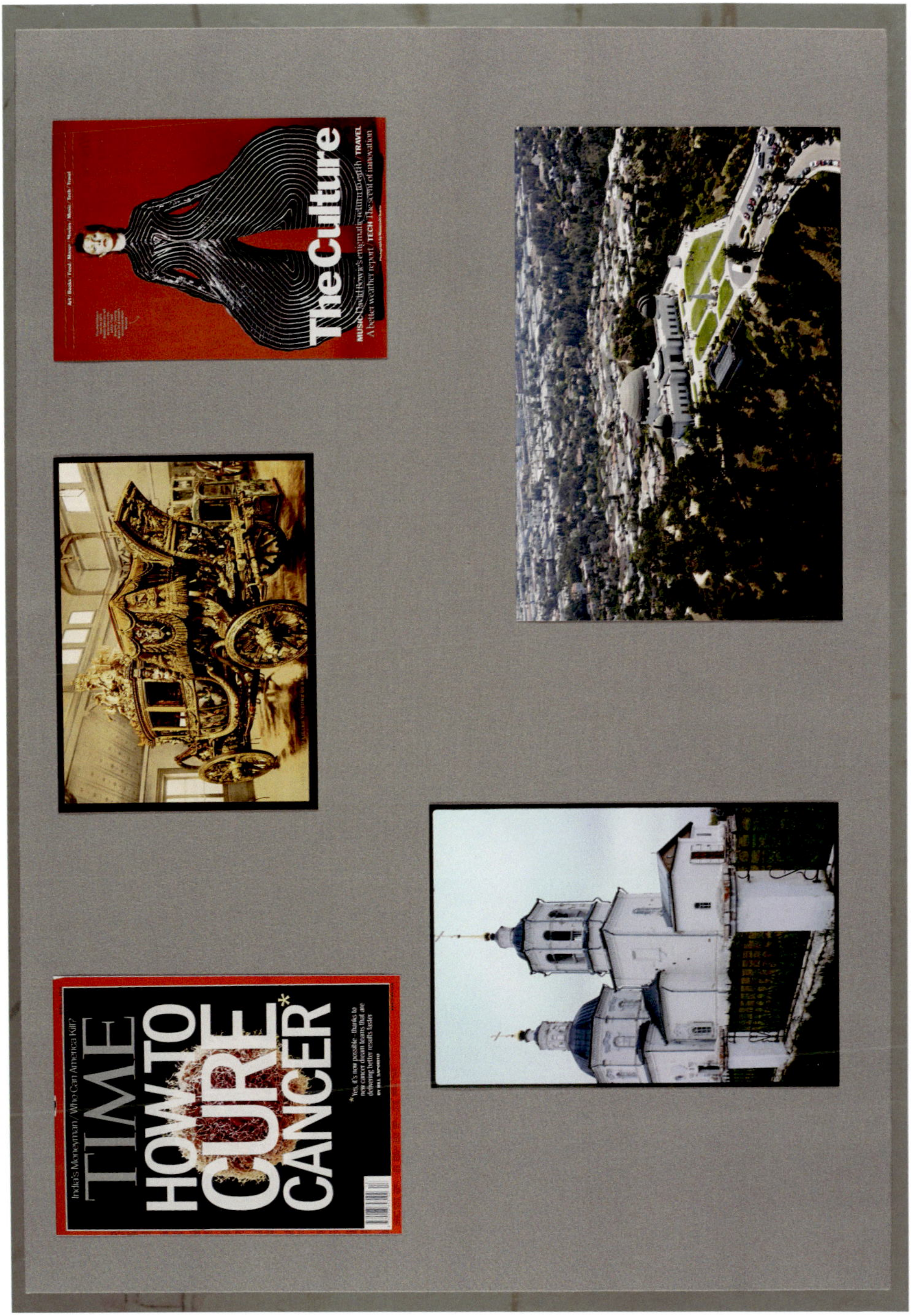

round dominant shapes (plate 3) [MA]

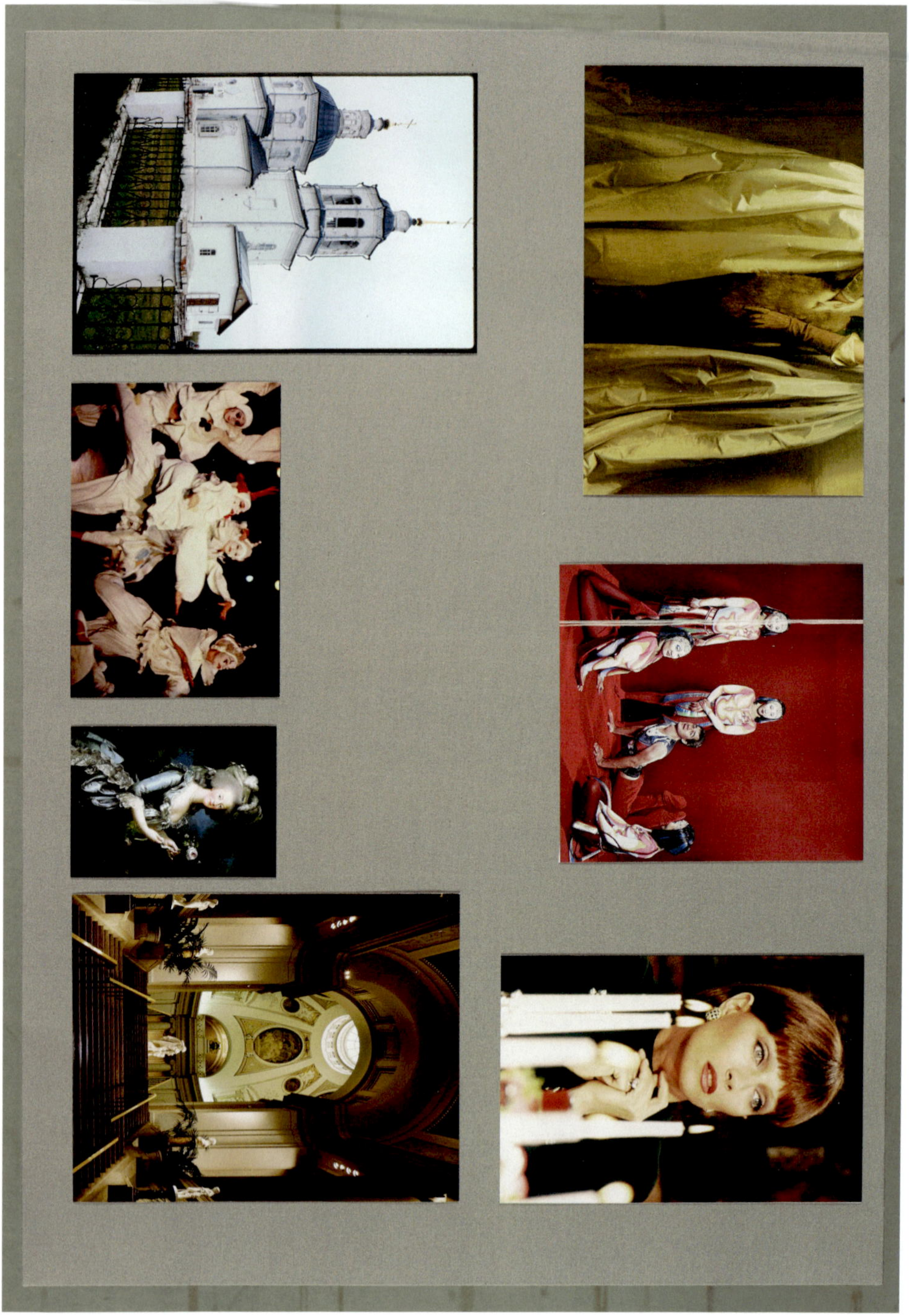

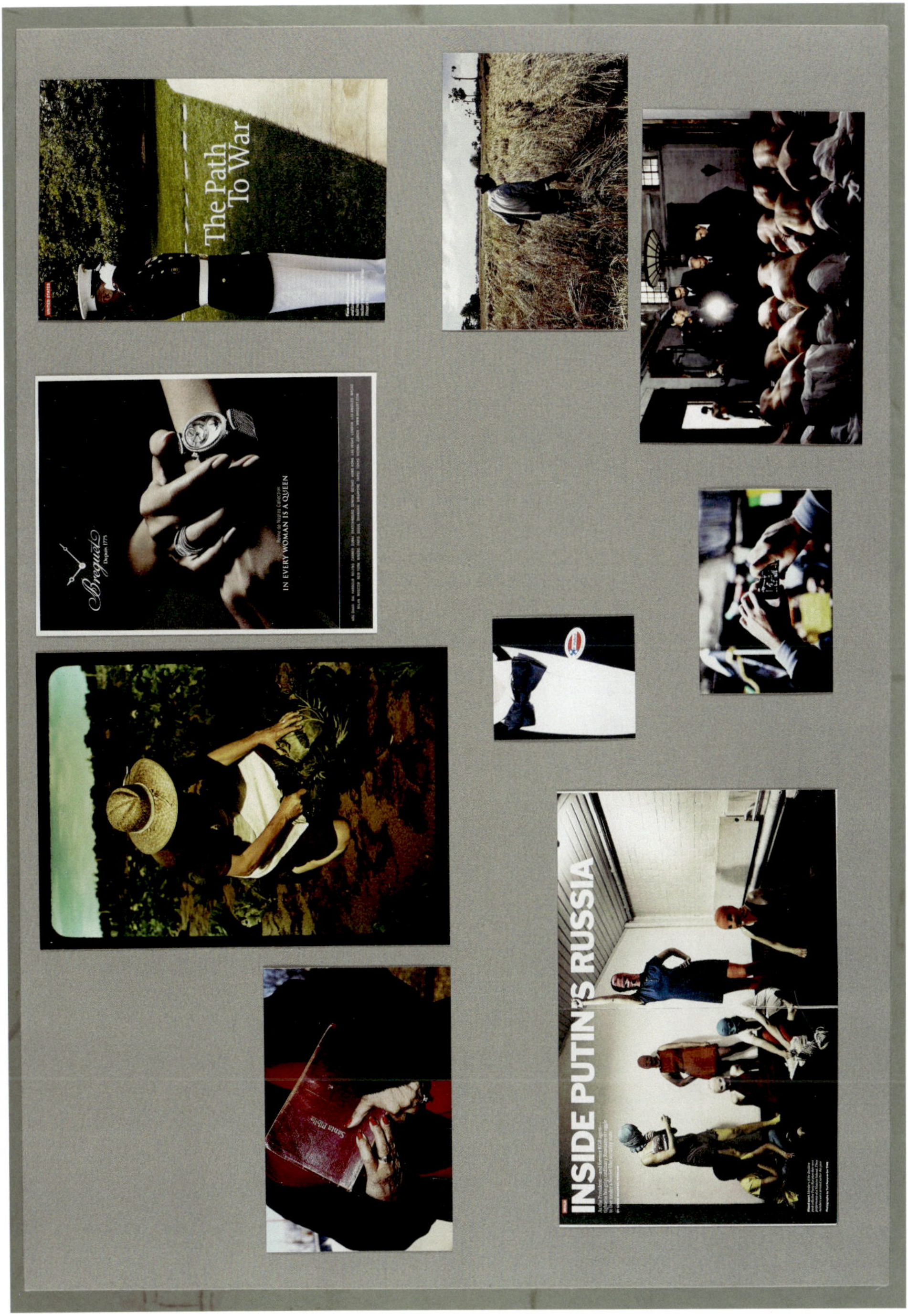
The Path To War
Breguet
Depuis 1775
IN EVERY WOMAN IS A QUEEN
INSIDE PUTIN'S RUSSIA

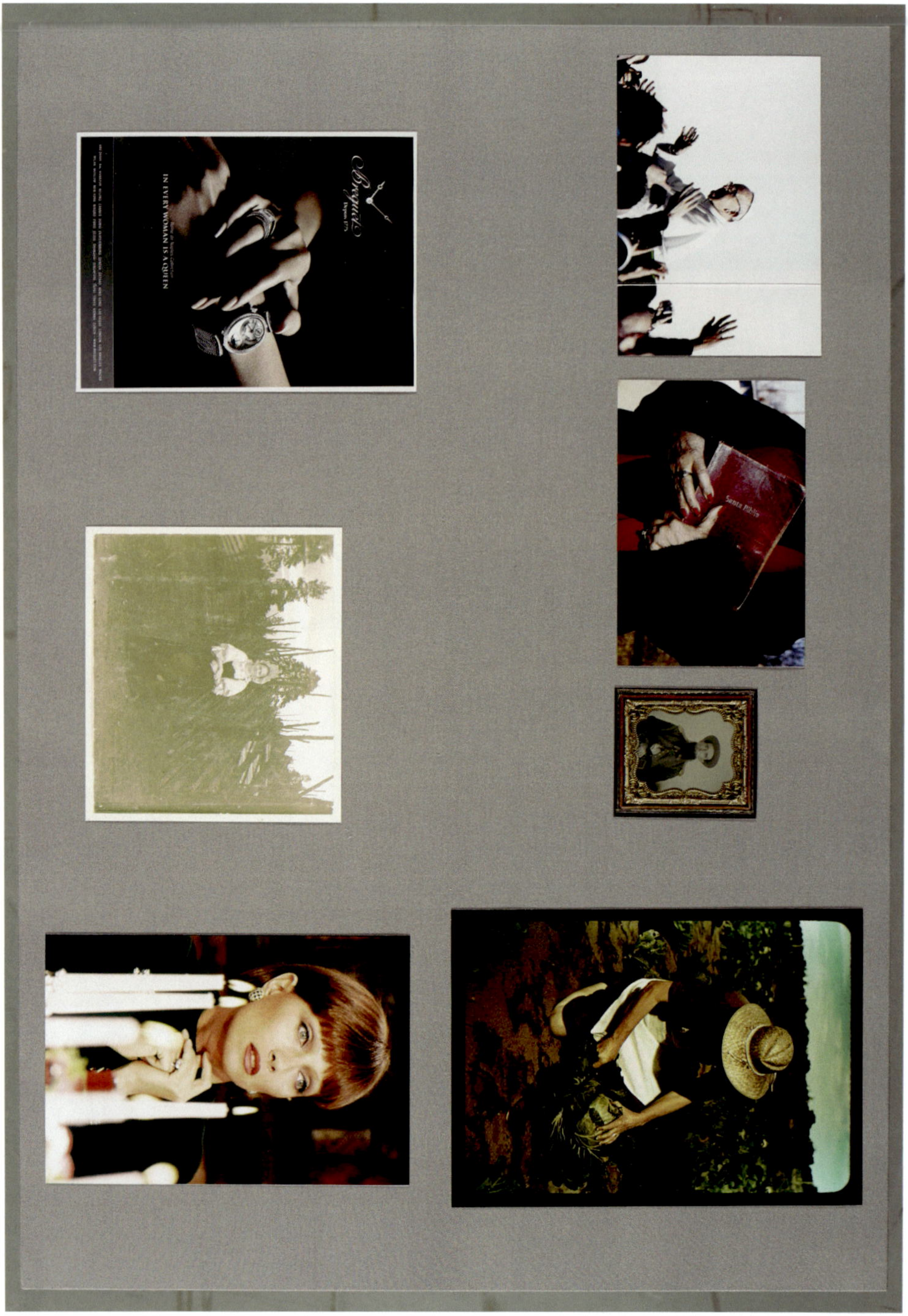
IN EVERY WOMAN IS A QUEEN
Santa Biblia

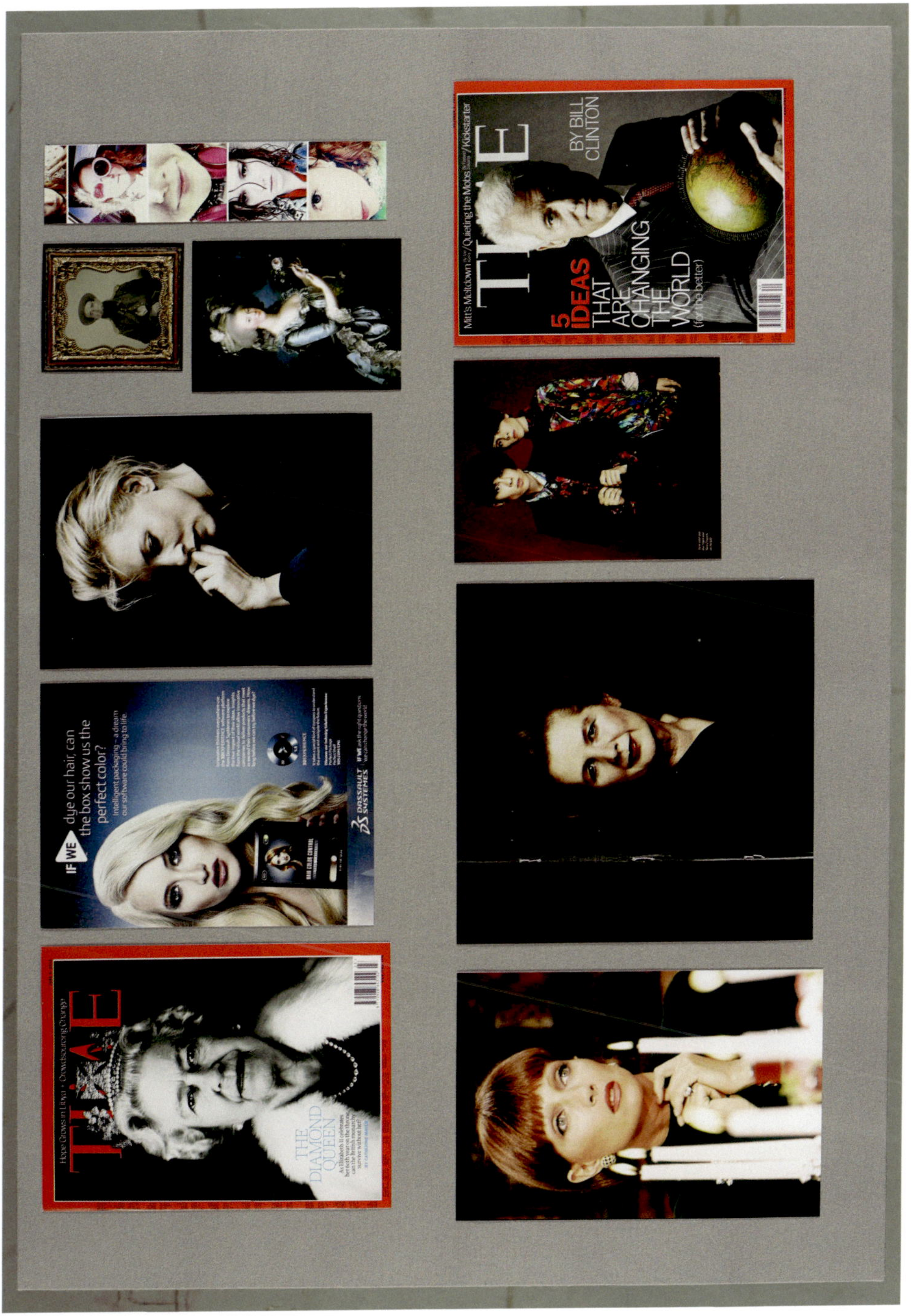
TIME
Mitt's Meltdown / Quieting the Mobs / Kickstarter
BY BILL CLINTON
5 IDEAS THAT ARE CHANGING THE WORLD
(for the better)
IF WE dye our hair, can the box show us the perfect color?
Intelligent packaging – a dream our software could bring to life.
DASSAULT SYSTEMES
TIME
Hope Grows in Libya • Crowdsourcing Change
THE DIAMOND QUEEN

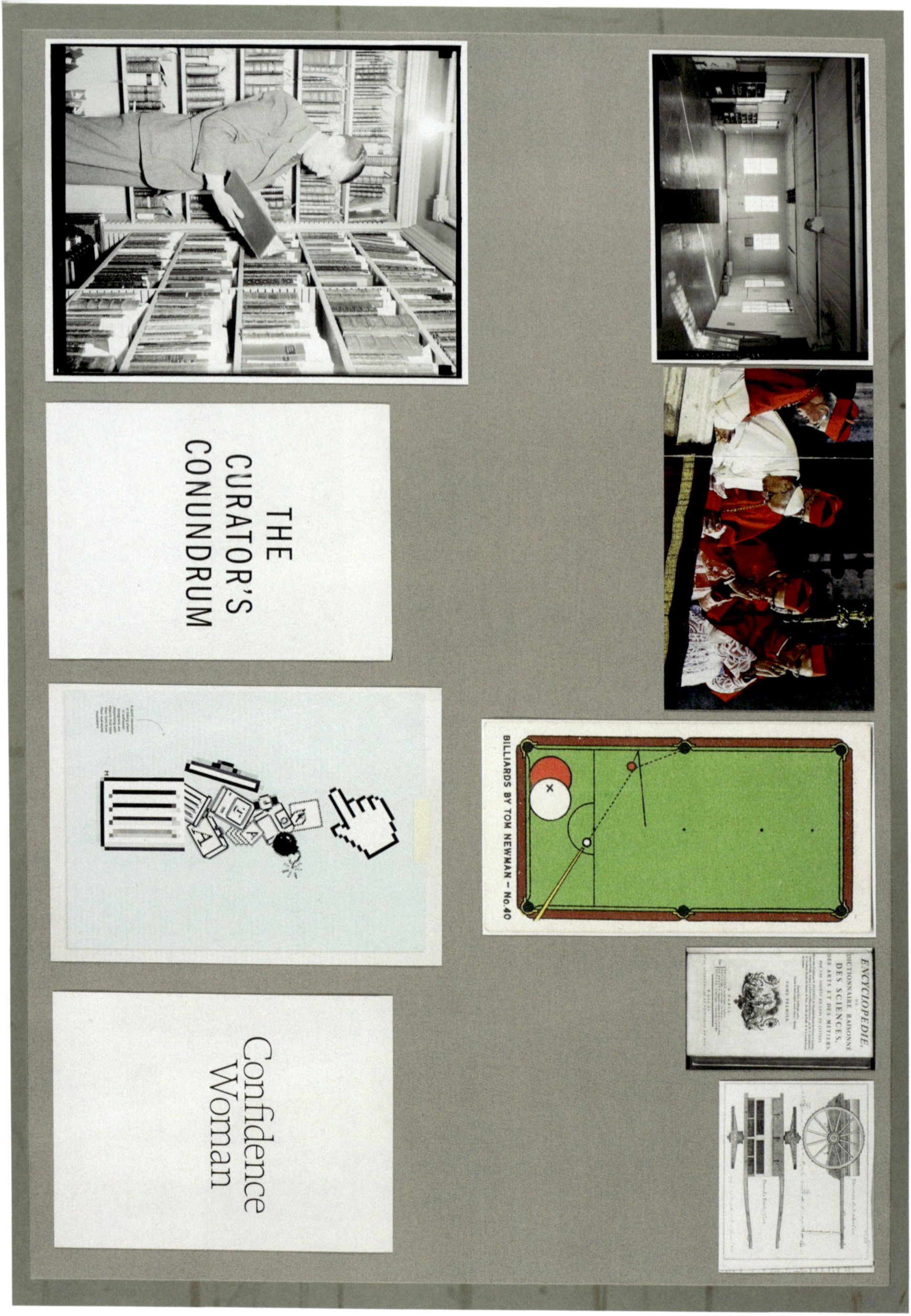
THE CURATOR'S CONUNDRUM
Confidence Woman
BILLIARDS BY TOM NEWMAN – No.40
ENCYCLOPEDIE,
DICTIONNAIRE RAISONNE
DES SCIENCES,
DES ARTS ET DES METIERS,

ENGLISH TRANSLATIONS

> '[...] if photography is a mapping of bodies in time and space, then it is also a production of both those bodies and modernity's particular conception of the time-space continuum.'
> – Geoffrey Batchen[1]

Christina Irrgang

ENCOUNTERING VISUAL TOTALITY

On the work of Fari Shams

We communicate through language and images. Yet, neither language nor images adhere to the same system, not even when they function within the same cultural milieu. The ambiguity of the visual and linguistic reveals the complexity of systems through which language and images become accessible in their respective contexts, and through which they can be ordered. An order is never absolute because it too is bound by a systematic rule which varies from situation to situation. A system of order only leads to a synthesis if it creates structure itself within its respective context, that is to say, if it sustains and reinforces the logic of the situation. In its essence, order is never hierarchical: instead, it is intrinsically abstract, even reflexive. The system which it classifies however, forms a hierarchy thereby undermining the democratic character of the order. Classification is defined by a decision maker; therefore, its character is subjective. But the subjective decision accords to a given structure. Systems of order are always, and at the same time, never true.

Language and images, literary and scientific texts, writing and magazines, image archives and spaces that follow an order are the parameters of Fari Shams' work. The observation of relationships between image and text, the narrative order and alignment of image, and language constitute a recurrent theme in her oeuvre. Befittingly, the installation that was the reason for and place of our first encounter in 2012 was entitled *The Order of Things*. The piece consists of a sound installation, and an artist book where Alain Robbe Grillet's text *THREE REFLECTED VISIONS - The Dressmaker's Dummy* is appropriated through language, illustration, reproduction, and photographic re-enactment in search of the space which it defines. In the exhibition space[2] I was surrounded by a recorded voice. The narration encircled me scenically: descriptions of an absent room encountered within the real room in which I found myself, its coordinates defined by words. Through its inward folding and outward extending pages the artist book *reflections on Three reflected Images - The Dressmaker's Dummy* mirrors and constructs the room further in the midst of photographic situations, and analytical notes on Robbe Grillet's text augmenting, and prismatically expanding, the spectrum of its configuration.

Fari Shams dismantles systems of order, and through the process of duplication generates counter-images "Gegenbilder" that expose the condition of the pictorial. An autonomy with respect to the camera as apparatus "Apparative Autonomie"[3] is inherent in her work: photography is a formative element but the artist synthesises the photographic with particular attention to its image-making properties. In Vilém Flusser's words, Shams acts 'towards a philosophy of photography', conscious of the question of freedom within a context[4] that is initiated through the photographic act itself.

If existence oscillates between chaos on the one hand and frameworks defined by an apparatus on the other, how can we still find freedom and locate ourselves or respectively give ourselves space to exist? 'Freedom is playing against the Apparatus'.[5]

The medium of the book often serves the artist as a means of reflection and presentation as in the work *European Civilization, Peter the Great, and the Order of Things* (2014), which is the point of departure, and subject of the following discussion. The foundation of the work is established through four books which present permutations of a fixed set of photographic images under different systems of classification. The sources of the photographic reproductions are analogue and digital; they are metaphors for the quotidian and the popular. Part of this material consists of excerpts from 2012 issues of *TIME* Magazine. Shams supplements these excerpts (individual photographs, spreads, advertisements, typography, illustrations or magazine covers) with a further selection of images from the Prints & Photographs Online Catalogue of the Library of Congress' archive, the world's largest library based in Washington, D.C. There are a total of 145 images that Fari Shams subsequently digitised and then re-contextualised through different methods and media. There is a noticeboard, which documents the 145 images like the members of an alphabet. Within the exhibition space itself these images are laid out under different systems of classification with the noticeboard always serving as the backdrop and source of the permutations of images. A projection shows a selection of 40 different plates of image combinations. A series of table presentations in turn present texts, plates of images, and the aforementioned books. These books are the focus of the following section as they demonstrate Fari Shams' continuously shifting visual system through four applied methods.

The first book features the 145 images in alphabetical order, based on their corresponding names or captions. In the second volume Shams orders the sourced images according to Denis Diderot's *Map of the System of Human Knowledge* (1750), while the third volume applies an ethnographic-botanical classification based on Michel Adanson's *Familles naturelles des plantes* (1763, see page 74). The fourth volume juxtaposes selected image pairs from each of the three systems. The selection of 145 images refers back to a list of keywords that Fari Shams selected from a lecture by John Merriman on *Peter the Great,* (from which the title of the piece is also derived): *European Civilization 1648-1945.* The lecture by the historian Merriman held at Yale University is part of a series but in Fari Shams' installation it takes on the role of a kind of colophon that functions like an index to the work *European Civilization, Peter the Great, and the Order of Things* since the keywords act as the point of departure for the work.

The reformist ideas of Peter the Great that looked towards western examples in order to rebuild a modern, enlightened Russian State are in the work *European Civilization, Peter the Great and the Order of Things* in keeping with the allegorical, photographic mediation of western values via western channels of visual communication. While Peter the Great (1672-1725) lived in a time when multiple images were en vogue as new forms of observation, as for example in the representations of the Dutch Picture Gallery by David Teniers, we currently negotiate our way through the cosmos based almost exclusively on communication through dialogical images. Photographs function as interfaces between capitalism and control. They control our consciousness and capitalistic behaviour, or, as in the words of Geoffrey Batchen, '[...] the meaning of every photograph is imbricated within broader social and political forces.'[6] How then do the values mediated as pictorial systems conversely re-enter capitalist society? Shams shifts the perspective on contemporary, social, political, and cultural implications with her photographic cross-section of one year of the *TIME* Magazine while simultaneously challenging the values embodied and transferred by the digital library archive. 'What is the photograph on the inside before it enters a specific historical and political context?'[7] This question posed by Geoffrey Batchen is also raised here.

With her critical investigation of images, Fari Shams works to unravel her subject in a way that recalls the philosophical and theoretical analysis of Michel Foucault in *The Order of Things*. Foucault's excavation of words and things sets up a framework where thinking is represented as being part of a network. If we assume that we increasingly think through images then such a network is positioned in Shams' work as a socially and culturally determined apparatus responsible for the production of images, i.e. for the production of thought.

In this context Shams' four-part book *European Civilization, Peter the Great and the Order of Things* takes on the function of a heterotopia.[8] It establishes a fixed position from which to observe a constant rendering of the images in specific combinations under four different mechanisms. Hence the artist undertakes an archaeological organisation of these globally distributed photographic images and examines their cultural signification by repeatedly reassembling them. Initially Fari Shams refers to Diderot's *Map of the System of Human Knowledge*, in which human knowledge is broken down into the categories of *memory*, *reason* and *imagination*, respectively through history, philosophy and poetry. Thus *memory*, *reason* and *imagination* come to constitute categories for Shams' index of images, reflecting on civilization, methods of communication and the formation of (photographic) narratives. The images in *European Civilization, Peter the Great, and the Order of Things* therefore appear as archetypes of experience, recognising, judging and acting.[9] The artist challenges these archetypes by performing their very construction herself through the assignment of categories: they organise what exists within their own boundaries and exclude what cannot be integrated.[10] Consequently photography becomes a medium of storage, of inventory, order, and systematisation:[11] an encyclopedia, which on the one hand represents distinct interrelationships between groups of images but on the other hand one which quickly mutates according to a new context under different parameters. Taken together as a whole, the classification systems that Shams refers to constitute a system of critical scrutiny.

Thus the recurrence of an image and its repositioning serve Fari Shams both as structure and method. Book III is exceptional in this sense with its recourse to Adanson's method for the classification of plants in Senegal under the title *Familles naturelles des plantes* published in 1763. Shams applies Adanson's method to the 145 images in the alphabetical order they find themselves in the first book by sequentially describing each without repeating any characteristic already mentioned. This process gives rise to characteristics that distinguish the set of 145 images and form the foundation for classifying them. Thus the descriptions form the categories that assemble groups of images on plates in volume III.

The images adhere to a system based on language, but their presentation eludes any kind of verbalisation. Here language and image are connected together in a type of 'double bind': they are mutually dependent; however, in their representation they become mutually exclusive. A binary ideology inherent in the visual arises: a visual antagonism where image and counter-image act against each other;[12] a tableau like language, with reference to Foucault, 'now language is image.'[13] However, according to Vilém Flusser the technical image is always exclusively based on language or a popular linguistic apparatus, and in fact follows a post-alphabetic logic (code). Finally, in its appropriation here, Adanson's method appears not only as a tautology but also as a 'mis en abyme' — an image within an image, that always contains itself.

In *European Civilization, Peter the Great, and the Order of Things* Fari Shams has generated an atlas of images that without a doubt conceptually and aesthetically echoes the formal characteristics of the *Mnemosyne Atlas* of Aby Warburg with its analytical stretched fabric plates and in particular the textured background on which the images are placed. But at the same time, this work is a reader on the politics of the image. Its data encompass an arbitrary surrogate of archival images accumulated online together with reproductions from the issues of the news magazine *TIME* from 2012, and on which broad sections of the world population subjectively base their world view after they have been adapted in accordance with specific methods and standards. Susan Sontag writes: 'It is always an image that someone chose; to photograph is to frame, and to frame is to exclude.'[14] Judith Butler takes this thought a step further: 'It is not necessary to have a caption or narrative at work to recognise that a political background is being explicitly formulated and extended through the frame (author's note: the choice of the cropped image)'[15] — in the context of photography, as well as in the scope of image editing or the structure of an archive. Fari Shams revives this process, makes editorial decisions, and produces a dialectic tension through fragmentation and repositioning — especially in the fourth volume of the publication in which she presents selected image pairs. Individual images enter into a comparative relationship, yet Shams reframes the images repeatedly, dialogically mobilising them into new constellations. They form a dialectic, in which 'each element functions as a separate subject of speech,'[16] yet together they constitute a narrative based on seriality. 'When things are repeated,' Hans Peter Feldmann commented, referring to photographic images, 'a generality arises that has more specificity than a single image by itself could have.'[17] The repetition of images multiplies the potential ways of seeing them. The images selected by the artist form a subjective data pool that, apart from its finite microsystem, can at the same time be contrasted to the space of the internet in the sense that a technical function (search engine) — coupled with subjective search parameters — selectively retrieves images and then systematically recombines them. But here the disposable nature of images is blocked by a deliberately formulated selection. Shams' four part book formats 'the oscillation of images between digital space and the space of the book'[18], while at the same time negotiating the boundaries between analogue and digital archives within the books and also in the exhibition space in the form of a publication and projection. 'Photography will [...] lose its power as a privileged conveyor of information. Given the proliferation of digital images that look exactly like photographs, photography may even be robbed of its cultural identity as a distinctive medium,'[19] writes Geoffrey Batchen. Accordingly Fari Shams reflects on the visual matrix of a global archive on a meta-media level by establishing a systematisation and by enforcing a 'controlled' perception between orientation and chaos — as a temporary matrix.[20]

Constellations and alliances arise, flipping the contextual signification of images and building new contexts that address such issues as, among others, church and military, world orders and spaces of action, technology and marketing, and gender and clichés. The artist therefore works within the boundaries of time and memory, in much the same way that they were described by Diderot in the *Map of the System of Human Knowledge*. Which images are the ones that fix themselves in memory and which transported gestures fall into oblivion? The material and the cultural overlap: 'Photography as something that is simultaneously material and cultural, manifested as much in the attributes of the photographic object as in its contextualisation. Philosophy has a word for all this: deconstruction.'[21]

Deconstruction finally becomes most evident in the selection of only 40 plates from the total of 212 for the projection in the exhibition. While the four part book as an image encyclopedia always refers back to a complete image set, namely the set of 145, the projection functions in its deliberate selection as the fragmentation of this body of images. The projection becomes a metaphor for incompleteness, for the loss of information and data. It points to the porosity of any given system, the fragility of representation. It becomes the paraphrase of the four part book.

The archive, its re-configuration as well as its incompleteness, is a subject matter that Fari Shams repeatedly returns to in her work. The project that consequently gave rise to the artist book with the same title, *The Concise Companion to Art History written by Ingo Müller and Gerd Schneider* (2014) is an archive of image data that Shams found in the out-of-date archive of glass slides at the Art Academy in Düsseldorf and which she subsequently digitally reconstructed with the help of internet search engines. Here the gaps and the discontinuity of an alphabetical or thematic order became structurally formative parameters for the work as this was no longer evident in the physical, fragmentary slide archive. The deconstruction and reconstruction of the archive thus became the point of departure for Fari Shams' publication. And in this work it is also demonstrated: in de- and reconstruction, the concept of the archive collapses when viewed as a fragment. 'That which survives in the archives does so by chance. Disappearance is the rule,'[22] Susan Buck-Morss comments on the ephemerality of archives, defining chance as a regulating factor. Shams' work acknowledges that categorisation and methodology are essential for the analytic evaluation of images, but that categorisation and methodology can lead to consequences, such as disappearance: a mechanism that in the present time repeats itself in the virtual space of the internet — with the subjective 'encyclopedia' as a result. In her work, Fari Shams reflects the fragmentary nature of the contemporary perception of images that, although steadily growing in number, are at the same time identified by determined criteria of selection.

Here, with *European Civilization, Peter the Great, and the Order of Things*, the body of the archive represents an index of images located between populism and historicity,[23] that is rooted in a process of pre-narrative censorship, and appropriated within the projection and the four-part book as a post-narrative sequence. The images establish a photographic dispositif. Shams' image plates reflect a visual totality spanning over the technical reproduction of images through different channels of communication and media, from photographic reproductions, the moving image, and image-based mediums through to online digital images. Technical images with reference to Vilém Flusser's 'techno-images' have never been in wider circulation than today. But this circulation of visual totality is interrupted by discontinuities that become the field of action for the artist. Fari Shams positions the abundance of images together with the continually superimposed authorship they bear into a new discursive sphere of consideration with an archaeological, conceptual approach: with coherence she reveals discontinuities, with absolute perfection the incomplete and the porous, and with precision the absurd. She plays with the mechanisms of the systems she appropriates — against the system. ●

1 – Geoffrey Batchen, *Each Wild Idea: Writing, Photography, History* (Cambridge: MIT Press, 2002), p. 23.

2 – Baustelle Schaustelle, Essen (12th April -10th May 2013).

3 – Expression used by Gertrud Koch in her text: 'Tun oder so tun als ob? – alternative Strategien des Filmischen', in Gertrud Koch and Christiane Voss (eds), *Es ist, als ob – Fiktionalität in Philosophie, Film- und Medienwissenschaft* (Munich: Fink, 2009), p. 139.

4 – Cf. Vilém Flusser, *Towards a Philosophy of Photography*, trans. Anthony Mathews (London: Reaktion Books, 2000), p. 79.

5 – Flusser 2000, p. 80.

6 – Batchen 2002, IX.

7 – Ibid.

8 – Cf. Michael Hagner's considerations of photo books and heterotopia: 'The latter emerges as an alternative space separate from the web, ingesting, processing, and transforming its elements, opening to let the digital stream in and then closing again, bringing together what would seem utterly incompatible. The heterotopias Foucault described — gardens, attics, wigwams, ships — are not infinitely large, but, on the contrary, tightly constrained; the book, too, is a delimited space.' Michael Hagner, 'The Photobook, Post-Digital', *Texte zur Kunst – Photography*, 99, (September 2015), p. 116.

9 – Cf. Flusser 2011, p. 34.

10 – Cf. Herta Wolf, 'Positivismus, Historismus, Fotografie – Zu verschiedenen Aspekten der Gleichsetzung von Geschichte und Fotografie', *Fotografiegeschichte*, 63, (1997), p. 36.

11 – Ibid., p. 38.

12 – Derived from the title: *Bild gegen Bild – Image Counter Image*, exhib. cat. for the eponymous exhibition and symposium, Haus der Kunst, Munich (Cologne: Walther König, 2012).

13 – 'Then, [in the 18th century] it was a matter of dividing nature up by means of a constant table of identities and differences for which language provided a primary, approximative, and rectifiable grid; now, language is image, [...]', in Michel Foucault, *The Order of Things* (London: Routledge, 2005), p. 323.

14 – Susan Sonntag, *Regarding the Pain of Others* (London: Penguin Books, 2003), p. 41.

15 – Judith Butler, 'Torture and the Ethics of Photography', *Environment and Planning D: Society and Space*, 25 (2007), p. 952.

16 – Peter Osborne, 'The Distributed Image', *Texte zur Kunst – Photography*, 99 (September 2015), p. 80.

17 – Hans-Peter Feldmann in conversation with Kasper König, in Hans-Peter Feldmann: *Another Book*, exhib. cat., (ed.) Helena Taty, (London: Koenig, 2010), supplement, p. 11. The interview was first published in *Frieze Magazine*, May 2005.

18 – Cf. Michael Hagner, 'The Photobook, Postdigital', *Texte zur Kunst – Photography*, 99 (September 2015), p. 115.

19 – Batchen 2002, p. 129.

20 – Cf. Susan Buck-Morss, 'The temporal matrix in which truth is embedded, essentially transient, is the criterion for critical judgment — a difficult idea, because it goes against conventional procedures that narrate history sequentially and at a distance. In view of the fleeting nature of truth, any attempt at permanence of historical interpretation leads to error. [...] Past events cannot provide a key to the present unless they are radically separated from a direct lineage of inheritance.' Susan Buck-Morss, 'The Gift of the Past, Constellations', in documenta 13, *The Book of Books* (Ostfildern: Hatje Cantz, 2012), p. 96/97.

21 – Batchen 2002, IX.

22 – Buck-Morss (ibid.), p. 94.

23 – '[...] Poetry leads to the same place. Blending and fusion of separate objects. It leads us to death and through death to continuity. Photographs have laid down these routes [sic!]. Made out of dung. Created by ideologies. Archives of images, representative images, which encapsulate common ideas of significance. Not piles but poster-ready pools. Oceans. The Sun matched with the Sea', Arranged by Geoffrey Farmer, in Tobias Spichtig and Fabian Schöneich (ed.), *Blue, Red, and Green*, (Berlin: Sternberg Press, 2012) p. 6. Cf. Geoffrey Farmer's investigation of photographic ideologies, for instance based on Life magazine in his piece 'Leaves of Grass' (2012).

Daniela Stöppel

PETER THE GREAT AND THE ORDER OF HIS WORLD

With the title *European Civilization, Peter the Great and the Order of Things* Fari Shams refers explicitly to Michel Foucault's treatise *Les mots et les choses* (1966), as well as the Russian Czar Peter the Great (1672-1725), whose reforms modernised the Russian state in accordance with Western models and, beginning in 1703 with the help of foreign architects, brought Saint Petersburg out from under the ashes through a series of aggressive social reforms. Under his reign, the reorientation of the Russian Empire resulted in a spelling reform, the establishment of systematically organised art and natural history collections, a great literacy campaign, and other ambitious projects. Fari Shams became interested in Peter the Great after a visit to Russia in 2013.

The reform efforts of Peter the Great manifest themselves distinctly within the inherent order established in the urban planning of Saint Petersburg. The Russian symbolist Andrei Bely described it in his 1905 novel *Petersburg* as defined by the straight axis of Nevsky Prospect: 'All Petersburg is the infinity of a prospect raised to the power of n.'[1] Even the "lines", being the parallel running streets of Vasilyevsky Island that are referred to in this way to this day, preserve 'the memory of Petrine Petersburg, Peter's City'.[2]

One of the protagonists of the novel, the high-ranking officer Apollon Apollonovich, to whom the correct arrangement of the world was of great concern for professional reasons, felt an overwhelming desire during a coach ride for 'blackish grey cubes of houses running like a winding coil on every prospekt and spanning the entire surface of the globe. The earth, encircled by these prospekts that embody the law of the straight line, would intersect infinity. Moreover, this network of parallel prospekts would be bisected by a second network of parallel prospekts and this system of squares and cubes would span over the darkest depths of the universe. (...).'[3]

The square grid would therefore emanate from Nevsky Prospect as a network and extend itself over the entire world. In the novel, the character of the high-ranking civil servant Apollon Apollonovich adopts the order that Peter set out for St Petersburg as a world order. The name Apollon Apollonovich is to be understood as the opposite to the Dionysian principle. The symbolist Alexander Benois already described Saint Petersburg in 1902 as "Apollonian", since it embodied the 'spirit of order, the spirit of the perfect form of life'[4], a city that would not tolerate 'general untidiness'. Bely indicates that Apollonovich even applied this spirit of order to his own domestic environment: 'Apollon Apollonovich engaged himself only once with the trivial aspects of life: one day he revised the contents of his house, systematically registered each item and accordingly labelled the drawers of a cabinet with alphabetical letters to organise them. The four sides of each drawer were additionally labelled north, south, east and west appropriately. As Apollon Apollonovich put his spectacles away he noted down the following in fine handwriting in his register and gave it to his Butler: spectacles, shelf b, NE, meaning North East.'[5]

The cartographic, rectilinear coordinate system of the urban layout of Saint Petersburg translates itself in Apollon Apollonovich's housekeeping as a microstructure that follows the rationale of Peter the Great's order.

The bureaucracy of the Russian tsardom, born in the spirit of absolutism that ingrained itself architecturally in the city of civil servants and soldiers of Saint Petersburg, began to falter during the revolution of 1905, the period covered in Bely's novel. Bely expresses this revolution through a literary collision between the grid system and amorphous, formless structures, thereby emphasising the instability of the new world order but at the same time establishing a utopian spirit born within the resulting cracks of that space, developing as non euclidean forms. The formlessness of the new anarchistic movement paved the way to a new world — overcoming all order. Bely saw this less as a new world order and more as a withdrawal from order. With reference to European civilization in general, this is simply intended by the author to offer another perspective. The principle of disorder or non-order will be addressed in the coming pages.

Like most systems, Saint Petersburg is an abstract formation, a conception out of nothing, an a priori configuration, a creation of the mind. Nevsky Prospect runs in the form of a straight line from the Admiralty to the Alexander Nevsky monastery. As an artificial perspective (this is another way the streets of Saint Petersburg are referred to) it creates an additional coordinate system that acts as a space of power and representation.

While the great systems of classification of the French tradition including Diderot and d'Alembert's *Encyclopaedia* (from 1751) could qualify even today as projects of the Enlightenment, this proves to be more problematic in the case of Peter's project. His reform efforts were often carried out with too much force, as instruments of power, not only to stabilise political power but in addition to extend it. And this was the only way that it was possible to build Saint Petersburg on the Finnish swampy marshlands, because, in accordance with the Ukase, the serfs could be subjected to forced conditions of labour and taxation. The contradictions of the Enlightenment are clear to see when looking at the reforms of Peter the Great, because, although they were not focused per se on autocracy and the authoritative exercise of power, they did in fact give rise to a separate system of power. Therefore there is perhaps no obvious contradiction between Enlightenment and despotism: in fact they are two sides of the same coin.

Fari Shams also starts her project with a subjective and consequently authorial gesture: she compiled her inventory of 145 images from a lecture by John Merriman about Peter the Great. This is a subjective decision but nevertheless is based on a standardised survey by Yale University — that can therefore claim a general validity. Keywords from the lecture are used to source the images from the 2012 issues of *TIME* Magazine and the online archive of the Library of Congress. Here too the issue of subjective decisions versus general significance comes into play. In the next step she tries to order them by applying the 145 images to different systems of classification. These are partly associated with established historical significance, as in Diderot's *Système Figuré des Connaissances Humaines* or the method of plant classification of Michel Adanson, and partly based entirely on personal decisions, as for example the intuitive placement of two images side by side.

In this way she contrasts the apparent objective nature of classification systems against subjective compilations of images: the transparency and ambiguity of the methods blend into one another. The parallelism of entirely different schemes of order indicate their arbitrariness and bring to mind snapshots of a thought process in permanent flux. And so Fari Shams creates ever new cross-sections that nevertheless ultimately make each other redundant.

Her concern with deconstruction is already evident in the choice of Diderot on the one hand and Adanson on the other. These two authors serve Foucault in *Les mots et les choses* to distinguish "system" and "method" from one another: while Diderot established a system based on the empirical collection of data, on the basis of which other observable phenomena could be classified, Adanson championed a structurally open and unrestricted classification, one in which new kinds of species could be defined as a result of the distinct differences in contrast to already established ones.

In Shams' work *European Civilization, Peter the Great and the Order of Things*, these methods are carried over and applied to images, which can be compared to a field test: which compilations come about through the schema of Diderot, and what do the groups of images look like when ordered according to Adanson's method? How do conceptual characteristics alter the order of a sequence in comparison to formal characteristics?

The first sequence of images follows an alphabetical order. To this end things (*choses*) need to be assigned words (*mots*), and here they are assigned the title of the image. The conventional relationship between things and their names is normally arbitrary, and in a way this is also the case with Shams where an arbitrary sequence arises that is based on the title of the image. Therefore, in the category of the letter G, one finds the following image titles: '41. Games, 42.Garden, 43.Golden boy, and 44.Griffith observatory LA'. The titles are neither formally nor contextually related. In addition the arranged images on the plate (from Super-Mario, a landscape garden, two footballers, and an observatory) do not have anything in common (see page 77).

The second sequence of images is determined according to Diderot's *Système Figuré des Connaissances Humaines.* The relationship between things (observable phenomena) and concepts is also the central focus here. By fitting many phenomena that he wanted to order into his conceptual tripartite classification system Diderot abstracted things from their names yet carried over conceptual categories with reference to the diverse nature of different forms of life. Fari Shams applied Diderot's tripartite system of *Memoire*, *Raison* and *Imagination* to her image index and found, for example, an Observatory under the category of *Reason.* Therefore she assigned contemporary photographic reproductions to one of Diderot's three conceptual categories and in doing so simultaneously pointed out the historicity of his a priori system. In this way the act of classifying itself does not seem to be separable from subjective decisions.

Unlike the alphabetical arrangements, however, the images classified according to Diderot's system seem to share certain formal characteristics within the same categories. Specific geometric forms seem to conform more to the category of *Reason* rather than *Imagination.* The grid described in Bely's novel, for example, if classified in this way would appear under the category of *Reason*. Peter's road system seems to manifest itself here in the form of a measurement grid over a human body. And the observatory mentioned above also finds itself in this system next to circular and dome-like configurations (see page 78).

And lastly, the method of Michel Adanson, rather than acting like a higher-level system, is a method of classification that gives rise to categories by applying a process of comparison. Shams uses this method by describing the characteristics of each of the images in their existing arbitrary alphabetical order, establishing keywords by comparing them to one another, and then using these keywords to re-group the images together once again. Central to Adanson's method is that only differences are recorded. In this way, for example, the group "round dominant shapes" is formed that interestingly underlines the formal characteristics of the images but moreover creates content-related relationships. The observatory in this system is now next to a cancer cell, a church and a striped overall among other elements that enable certain conclusions to be drawn about their form-content relationships (see page 79).

By working in this way, Shams uses a number of distinct approaches to get closer to the issue of whether form and content in fact correspond with one another, and which historical solutions were previously available to address this problem.

The personal approach to the material as well as the tautological overall construction of the project nevertheless emphasise the problem with any classification system that claims universal validity. The question of power is therefore not diminished in the multiple approaches to classification but rather becomes all the more visible. It does not seem possible to exit this infinite process of newly constructing the order of the world.

Finally, with reference to Daniil Kharms' text *A Treatise More or Less Following Emerson* (1939), it is possible, at least as a utopian goal, to withhold the possibility of any kind of order. In it he specifies the hierarchy of things through the example of giving:

> *The following kinds of gifts are imperfect gifts: for example, we give the birthday boy the lid for an inkwell. But where is the inkwell itself? Or we give the inkwell together with its lid. But where is the desk on which the inkwell must sit? If the birthday boy already has a desk, then the inkwell would be the perfect gift. Then, if the birthday boy has an inkwell, one may give him only the lid and that would be a perfect gift, as well. Decorations of the naked body, such as rings, bracelets, necklaces, etc. are always perfect gifts (if, of course, the birthday boy is not a cripple), or such presents as a stick, for instance, to the end of which has been attached a wooden ball and to the other end a wooden cube. Such a stick can be held in the hand, or, if one puts it down, then it doesn't matter at all where. Such a stick is no use for anything else.*[6]

An Apollonic coordinate system, or the comparative method of Adanson, seem not to be applicable to the stick with the appended wooden ball or cube. In this way order can be overcome on the basis of a new object-subject relationship. An idea that, as Shams shows us, can potentially also be applied to visual material like photographic reproduction. ●

1 – Andrei Bely, *Petersburg* (London: Penguin Classics, 1995), p. 17.

2 – Ibid., p. 84.

3 – Ibid., p. 78.

4 – See Karl Schlögel, *Petersburg. Das Laboratorium der Moderne.* 1909-1921 (Frankfurt am Main: Fischer Verlag, 2009), p. 29.

5 – Bely, *op.cit.*, p. 60.

6 – Daniil Kharms, 'A Treatise more or less following Emerson', in Matvei Yankelevich (ed.), *Today I Wrote Nothing* (New York: Ardis, 2009), p. 253.

CONTRIBUTORS

Morad Montazami (*1981)

has published several essays on artists such as Jeremy Deller, Francis Alÿs, Zineb Sedira, Éric Baudelaire, Walid Raad, Latif al-Ani, Bahman Mohassess, Mohammed Melehi, Faouzi Laatiris.
He is editor-in- chief of the Journal Zamân (Texts, images and documents) and director of Zamân Books, committed to exploring transnational studies of Arab, Asian and African modernities.
He was the co-curator of the exhibition *Unedited History: Iran 1960–2014*, Musée d'art moderne de la ville de Paris-MAXXI, Rome (2014-2015); as well as curator for *Volumes Fugitifs: Faouzi Laatiris et l'institut national des beaux-arts de Tétouan*, Musée Mohamed VI d'art moderne et contemporain in Rabat (2016).

Joseph Grigely (*1956)
School of the Art Institute of Chicago

is an artist and critical theorist. He has had solo exhibitions at the Whitney Museum of American Art; the MCA, Chicago; the Musée d'art Moderne in Paris; and the Douglas Hyde Gallery, Dublin; as well as the Whitney, Venice, Berlin, Istanbul and Sydney Bienniales. His books include *Textualterity: Art, Theory, and Textual Criticism* (1995), *Conversation Pieces* (1998), *Blueberry Surprise* (2006), *Exhibition Prosthetics* (2010), *MacLean 705* (2015), and *Oceans of Love: The Uncontainable Gregory Battcock* (2016), as well as essays on disability theory and body criticism. He has a D.Phil. from Oxford University and is Professor of Visual & Critical Studies at the School of the Art Institute of Chicago.

Daniela Stöppel (*1976)
Institute for Art History at LMU Munich

is Academic counselor at the Institute for Art History at the LMU in Munich and curator at Kunstraum München. She studied Art history, Sociology and Communications Science in Munich and obtained her PhD with a thesis on the visual system of signification in the avant-garde. Her main focus is on the art of the European avant-garde, nineteenth to twenty-first century history of painting, and Art Historiography.

Christina Irrgang (*1983)

lives and works as a Freelance Author in Wuppertal — Düsseldorf. She studied Art Research and Media Philosophy at the Karlsruhe University of Arts and Design, where she recently completed her PHD thesis on the photographer Heinrich Hoffmann in the context of the strategies of political image.

Fari Shams (*1976)

is an Iranian born British artist living and working in Düsseldorf and London. She studied at the School of the Art Institute of Chicago and at the Düsseldorf Art Academy. Her multidisciplinary practice involves issues concerning the production of knowledge, and the implications of isolating subjects and objects under observation for the purpose of understanding them. Her works are a result of daily experiences which bear witness to the human need for structural systems of organization and classification and the inherent inadequacy and incompleteness that characterise them. Her works have been recently shown in Centro per l'Arte Contemporanea Luigi Pecci, Prato, Italy; Museum Abteiberg, Mönchengladbach; apexart, New York; Kunstraum München; Maschinenhaus, Essen; and Museum Glaskasten, Marl, Germany.

IMPRINT

Fari Shams
European Civilization, Peter the Great and The Order of Things

Authors
Jospeh Grigely
Christina Irrgang
Morad Montazami
Daniela Stöppel

Photography
Fari Shams
Installation views, p. 50, 52:
Marion Benoit

Design Diderot Map of the System of Human Knowledge, p. 75
Matthias Wollgast

Book design
Edi Winarni

Translation
Fari Shams

Copyediting
John Wilks

Proofreading
John Wilks, Matthias Wollgast

Printing
optimal media

Published by
Spector Books
Harkortstraße 10
04107 Leipzig
www.spectorbooks.com

Distribution
Germany, Austria: GVA, Gemeinsame Verlagsauslieferung Göttingen GmbH&Co. KG, www.gva-verlage.de
Switzerland: AVA Verlagsauslieferung AG, www.ava.ch
France, Belgium: Interart Paris, www.interart.fr
UK: Central Books Ltd, www.centralbooks.com
USA, Canada, Central and South America, Africa, Asia: ARTBOOK/ D.A.P., www.artbook.com
South Korea: The Book Society, www.thebooksociety.org
Japan: twelvebooks, www.twelve-books.com
Australia, New Zealand: Perimeter Distribution, www.perimeterdistribution.com

First edition: 2020

Printed in Germany

ISBN 978-3-95905-420-1

Project funded by Kunststiftung NRW